God Is Not Your Problem

So why all the troubles?

Dr. Billy Ferg

God Is Not Your Problem
by Dr. Billy Ferg
Copyright ©2009 Dr. Billy Ferg

All rights reserved. This book is protected under the copyright laws of the United States of America. This book may not be copied or reprinted for commercial gain or profit. Unless otherwise identified, Scripture quotations are taken from the *Spirit-Filled Life Bible* Copyright ©1991 by Thomas Nelson, Inc. Scripture identified as Amp. is taken from: *The Amplified Bible*, Copyright ©1987 by The Zondervan Corporation and the Lockman Foundation. All are used by permission. All rights reserved.

ISBN 978-1-58169-307-2
For Worldwide Distribution
Printed in the U.S.A.

Axiom Press
P.O. Box 191540 • Mobile, AL 36619
800-367-8203

Table of Contents

Introduction v

1. Laying a Foundation of Truth 1

2. Who Is Responsible? 9

3. "But I Am Righteous!" 21

4. Fear Opens a Door 30

5. Accused Falsely 36

6. Grace, Mercy, and Judgment 44

7. The Mouthpiece of God 54

8. We Live By Our Words 61

9. God Shows Up 69

10. Repentance Is a Fresh Start 74

11. The Real Nature of God 82

12. The Fear of the Lord 90

13. What To Do When Trouble Comes 112

14. Summary 116

Introduction

Some years back, the Lord began to talk to me about Job. I was very surprised because He shared with me many unexpected things. He taught me things I had never understood or heard preached before.

We know that Job had many troubles in his life, not unlike you and me. The Lord taught me many things about where our troubles come from and how to be victorious over them in every situation. One thing that He made perfectly clear to me was that we never have to toil in life if we will live life *God's* way.

I know that whoever reads this book is going to find their way through whatever situation they are going through, and they will recognize that every good thing and every victory is from God. When we believe God's Word and faithfully apply it to our lives, our lives will never be the same.

Today begins a new direction for your life. Enjoy your life, for it is a gift from God and should not be taken lightly. Strive to live an extraordinary life, for you serve an awesome God!

CHAPTER ONE

Laying a Foundation of Truth

Establishing Doctrines

I am going to lay some foundations here that will flow throughout this book. To some people it will be common knowledge; to others it will be new, and that is all right. Every day I am learning about the awesome God I serve. It should be every believer's desire to know God and His loving, delivering power.

As we look at the book of Job, we realize that Job did not have a church to go to, and there was nothing written about God or the spirit realm. It was an amazing thing that he believed in God in the first place!

Job's knowledge of God was formed by hearing other people's opinions and ideas of God. His circle of influence and sources of information were mainly camel and donkey traders, sheep shearers, and caravans of vagabonds. This was how news and information traveled in those days. His opinions came from generations of tradition and by word-of-mouth. Back then people made up their own religion. They knew a little bit about tithing and making sacrifices, but it was mainly a "works" religion. They were trying to please God whom they had only heard of. Job did not know God personally. God did not talk to Job like He did to Noah, Moses, and Abraham. It was only out of a religious relationship that Job knew anything about God. That is why God did not hold this man's wrong doctrine and mind-sets against him.

In the first chapter of the book of James, it talks about the patience of Job. That was the nicest thing said about Job in the rest of the Bible—he had patience. He was remembered for patiently going through all he went through, but he was not remembered for accuracy in his understanding of God and spiritual matters.

However, Noah knew God as Judge of the living and the dead. He knew God as the God who had compassion on the righteous as well as the God who served justice on the unrighteous. Abraham knew God as the true and faithful God whose word could be believed at all times. He knew that He was a God in whom there was no variation or shadow of turning away from His followers. And Moses knew God as the Deliverer of His people, who would perform His promises even after more than 500 years had passed. He knew God as the God who would allow the destruction of the ungodly (Egyptians) to save and preserve His children, because God is a just God.

Today many people have made the book of Job a "sacred cow." They read the first few chapters and run with it. There are some churches that have used this book of the Bible almost exclusively to build their doctrines. The book of Job is an isolated book. There is no other book in the Bible that compares to it, confirms it, or endorses what is brought forth in it. It stands by itself. It is not wise to establish a doctrine in this way.

When doctrines are formed, there has to be harmony of the texts with other parts of the Bible. For instance, there is harmony between the Gospels; they are in agreement with each other and with the rest of the Bible. They all say basically the same thing. It is imperative that the whole Bible agrees with any doctrine being established.

Does the book of Job agree with the rest of the Bible? It is in the Bible, it has some truths and lessons to be learned because those things actually did happen to Job as told in the book, but not all of what is said is the truth. Some of what is said is out of nature with God and not in the flow of the Old Testament or New Testament. Please do not get confused by what I have just said, I will clarify it shortly.

1 Corinthians 3:1-4, "And I, brethren, could not speak to you as to spiritual people but as to carnal, as to babes in Christ. I fed you with milk and not with solid food; for until now you were not able to receive it, and even now you are still not able; for you are still carnal. For where there are envy, strife, and divisions among you, are you not carnal and behaving like mere men? For when one says, 'I am of Paul,' and another, 'I am of Apollos,' are you not carnal?"

Paul rebukes the first "denomination." Jesus did not start churches; He started and led the church! We are to be following Him as He leads, not following man's doctrine. Do not get caught up in religious pride. It is important to be a part of a church that preaches the whole Word, not just bits and pieces of it. I strongly endorse a good Bible-believing church with a pastor that is not afraid to preach the uncompromised Word of God because that is God's will for His followers. God has placed pastors over His flocks to lead, teach, and guide them as well as to bring them to a place of maturity.

God does not want us to be in darkness or confusion about His Word. He does not want us to be double-minded, either. It is His desire for us to know and operate in His truth. He wants us to see things His way, not man's way. He wants us in agreement with His Word.

When Paul wrote to the church at Corinth, he taught them about the spiritual gifts of the Holy Spirit.

1 Corinthians 12:1, "Now concerning spiritual gifts, brethren, I do not want you to be ignorant."

Paul knew that some Christians would resist the truth. This resistance is still present in some churches in the world today. Some churches are still uneducated concerning spiritual gifts, healing, and God's blessings. They do not understand the gifts and power of the Holy Spirit. God honors those who honor His Word. He does not back up *our* opinions or the fact that we were faithful to some particular church doctrine. He will honor and back the truth of His Word! That is why it is important that we know and accurately discern His Word.

1 Corinthians 14:38, "But if anyone is ignorant, let him be ignorant."

Paul is saying that some people will simply choose to be ignorant, and we will not be able to convince them to change their mind-set in our own power. This is still the situation with some people today. They *choose* to be ignorant of God's Word. They will follow after wrong doctrine because some theologian from their denomination interpreted the Bible his own way. When these people have been given over to the doctrines of demons or man's opinions, it is almost impossible to change their thinking about it; but nothing is impossible with God. We should never stop praying for people.

Here is an example of 1 Corinthians 14:38: I had a Jehovah's Witness come to my study one day. This man had been studying and attending the Jehovah's Witness hall for six years, but had not found the peace he was looking for in his life. He was searching for truth. I shared the *truth* about Jesus Christ being the only way to salvation. He prayed the sinner's prayer and received Jesus as his Lord and Savior. The man was touched and moved by the Holy Spirit and assured me that he would be in our church service the following Sunday. Do you know what happened? The next Sunday he went right back to the J.W. hall! Why?—because he *chose* to be ignorant. He chose to be a part of a cult and follow the doctrine of demons.

As I mentioned before, God is not impressed by man's opinions. We have to throw out the opinions of man and seek only *God's* understanding and meaning of His Word. If we truly fear (have a deep reverential awe, respect, and love for) God and are whole-hearted toward Him, our spirit man will know the truth when he hears it. We will have a deep-seated peace about the matter. Those who choose to be ignorant are lacking one or both of these virtues in their lives.

Get Wisdom and Discernment

> *James 1:5-8, "If any of you lacks wisdom, let him ask of God, who gives to all liberally and without reproach, and it will be given to him. But let him ask in faith, with no doubting, for he who doubts is like a wave of the sea driven and tossed by the wind. For let not that man suppose that he will receive anything from the Lord; he is a double-minded man, unstable in all his ways."*

James says that if we lack wisdom we can ask of God and He will answer. If

Jesus Christ is our Lord and Savior, then we have continual access to the Father. We can know all things that pertain to our life, and the mystery of God's Word will be revealed to us by the Holy Spirit.

> ***Ephesians 3:10-12,*** *"To the intent that now the manifold wisdom of God might be made known by the church to the principalities and powers in the heavenly places, according to the eternal purpose which He accomplished in Christ Jesus our Lord, in whom we have boldness and access with confidence through faith in Him."*

We have access, by the Holy Spirit, to the truth of God's Word, and it is our place as believers to share this truth with all boldness and confidence. But sometimes the church has failed to seek the Lord Jesus Christ and His Word or proclaim Him to a sin-laden world.

Some preachers today would rather take the easy way and preach puny messages about a small, weak Jesus. They deny His truth as well as the fact that we are to do what Jesus did while on the earth—*without exception!* These preachers do not fear God (have reverential awe and respect for Him). They are afraid of offending their congregation and taking the risk of some of them leaving. I hope these preachers change their ways if they know to whom they are ultimately accountable! Please do not get me wrong; I am not coming against preachers. I want to help them. I minister to over 1,200 pastors, evangelists, and teachers around the world, encouraging them to be righteous men and women of God. I encourage them to preach the uncompromised Word of God, knowing that is the only way to truly make a difference in this world and actually change people's lives.

In Ephesians 1 we see that we have been given an awesome inheritance through Jesus Christ:

> ***Ephesians 1:17-19,*** *"That the God of our Lord Jesus Christ, the Father of glory, may give to you the spirit of wisdom and revelation in the knowledge of Him, the eyes of your understanding being enlightened; that you may know what is the hope of His calling, what are the riches of the glory of His inheritance in the saints, and what is the exceeding greatness of His power toward us who believe, according to the working of His mighty power."*

In John 14, we see that Jesus told us in His own words that we are to be like Him.

> *John 14:12-14,* "*Most assuredly, I say to you, he who believes in Me, the works that I do he will do also; and greater works than these he will do, because I go to My Father. And whatever you ask in My name, that I will do, that the Father may be glorified in the Son. If you ask anything in My name, I will do it.*"

We need to allow this Scripture to become a profound, life-changing revelation to us. If we think about this a little, these verses confirm what is actually meant by the term "Christian." It means to be Christ-like. Did Jesus walk around murmuring and grumbling about all those people coming against Him? Did He walk around defeated, sick, in lack, and powerless over the devil? No! Then we do not have to either. However, we *do* have to make the choice whether we are going to be Christ-like or not. It does take effort, tenacity, and steadfastness in our relationship with the Father, but we *will* walk in victory and give glory to our heavenly Father if we stick to it.

Being Christ-like also takes having *"the spirit of wisdom and revelation in the knowledge of Him, the eyes of your understanding being enlightened"* (Ephesians 1:17-18). So, we have to realize that we do not have the needed wisdom and ask God for it; then He will give it to us liberally!

We need a lot of wisdom and discernment these days in order to differentiate God's truth from man's opinion. The Lord dropped a nugget of truth in my heart one day as I was praying about Job. He said, "Take a cup of sugar and a cup of salt. They are both good in themselves, but mix them together in a bowl and what do you have?" *Yuck!* You cannot cook with it, neither can you separate it. It is good for nothing.

God said, "That is what is happening in some churches today." They have man's doctrine on this side and God's truth on the other. They blend them together and get something unusable. Once they are blended, you cannot separate them. The mixture is good for nothing except to throw out. He says, "Keep the salt over here and the sugar over there, and use them for the right purposes." There are some ideas that man has that are good and helpful. There are some books and teachings from which one can glean good things. But when it comes to the Word of God, do not mix it up with *man's* ideas or opinions. Keep them separate.

God Is Love

I would like to share another word the Lord gave me concerning love. "Tell My people I love them. My love is above all other forces. It is more powerful than the mightiest power in the world. It is higher than the highest mountain. My love is constant. It does not change. My love is not like man's love. Man's love is conditional; it is based upon what someone can do for you. Man's love is based on what he can receive in return. You cannot drive My love away, because I *Am* love! I am the Creator of it. People have a difficult time understanding My love."

> *John 3:5-6, "Jesus answered, 'Most assuredly, I say to you, unless one is born of water and the Spirit, he cannot enter the kingdom of God. That which is born of the flesh is flesh, and that which is born of the Spirit is spirit.'"*

A sinner cannot help but sin because he is still only of the flesh. Only God's love is able to change a sinner and get him in right-standing with God. God's love then changes us so we do not live a willful life of sin. If we stumble, God is able to forgive us and receive us back into right-standing with Him. If we *willfully* sin it is because we are not abiding in Jesus Christ, and we have not made His love a part of us. When we understand how much God loves us, the last thing we would ever want to do is sin and hurt Him.

The Father talked to me about His only begotten Son, Jesus. He said, "My Son and I were very happy in heaven. We enjoyed being together. It was Our greatest delight, just as you enjoy being with your family. But We were saddened by man's sinful condition and his willingness to follow after the devil. So Jesus gave Himself as a ransom, to rescue all of mankind. He made the only way of escape for sinful man.

"Many a person has given their life for another; they have rescued someone from a fire, or they went to war to fight for a nation's freedom. That was done out of duty. But My Son, Jesus, gave His life for the whole world because He loved Me as well as the people of the world. He did it for Me because I loved the world and desired your fellowship. If people understood My love, they would find that whatever they ask for. I will give it to them." This is a beautiful word for today. We know that we are living under grace (God giving us things we do not deserve) and that we can receive God's love, but we see that there was grace in Old Testament times, too. It was grace that kept Adam and Eve from being totally destroyed for their rebellion. It was grace that brought the Israelites out of Egypt. It was grace that allowed that rebellious generation to die of natural causes during the forty years in the wilderness, instead of being utterly destroyed early in their journey to the Promised Land. It was God's grace that allowed King David, when caught in sin, to remain alive to go on serving God as Israel's king. God has always operated in grace.

> *2 Timothy 3:16-17, "All Scripture is given by inspiration of God, and is profitable for doctrine, for reproof, for correction, for instruction in righteousness, that the man of God may be complete, thoroughly equipped for every good work."*

With this essential foundation as to the character of God, now let's take a look at where our problems come from.

CHAPTER TWO

Who Is Responsible?

Inaccurate Portrayal of God

The book of Job is an important book and I'm glad it is in the Bible. If we read it with *God's* understanding, we will get a fresh love for Him and see that He could never bring this kind of terrible destruction on the people He loves.

The Lord did inspire the author of Job. However, He did not have the author write it from *God's* point of view. He had him write it from *Job's* viewpoint so we can see the mistakes that Job made, and not make the same ones. Unfortunately, for the most part, that has not happened. God wanted us to see that even back then there were gross misconceptions about Him. When read and understood through the wisdom of the Holy Spirit, we will avoid the pitfalls that Job got into.

The book of Job is an accurate account of what actually happened to Job in regard to his losses, the destruction, the conversations he had with his four friends, and the conversation that he had with God at the end of the book.

It is also an accurate account of what *Job* thought of God. However, the Lord made it perfectly clear to me that it was not an accurate account or portrayal of Him! Job had a real lack of understanding of how God or the devil works. He put God and the devil on an equal plane. We will talk more about that later.

The Lord allowed the book of Job to be included in the Bible in its present context, expecting those who read it to see Job's mistakes and misconceptions of God. However, many preachers and theologians missed Job's error and have made a "sacred cow" out of the book.

In the Old Testament they had tradition and superstition mixed in with their belief in God. Job was a religious man who thought highly of himself. He tried to explain what took place in his life, but initially it was an incorrect explanation. By the end of the book, he gets it right!

There is absolutely no relationship between God and the devil

> *Job 1:1-12, "There was a man in the land of Uz, whose name was Job; and that man was blameless and upright, and one who feared God and shunned evil. And seven sons and three daughters were born to him. Also, his possessions were seven thousand sheep, three thousand camels, five hundred yoke of oxen, five hundred female donkeys, and a very large household, so that this man was the greatest of all the people of the East.* (Author's note: Job's flocks and herds would be worth between $8 and $10 *million* in today's money—how is *that* for being a blessed man!)
>
> *Now his sons would go and feast in their houses, each on his appointed day, and would send and invite their three sisters to eat and drink with them. So it was, when the days of feasting had run their course, that Job would send and sanctify them, and he would rise early in the morning and offer burnt offerings according to the number of them all. For Job said, 'It may be that my sons have sinned and cursed God in their hearts.' Thus Job did regularly. "Now there was a day when the sons of God came to present themselves before the Lord, and Satan also came among them. And the Lord said to Satan, 'From where do you come?' So Satan answered the Lord and said, 'From going to and fro on the earth, and from walking back and forth on it.' Then the Lord said to Satan, 'Have you considered My servant Job, that there is none like him on the earth, a blameless and upright man, one who fears God and shuns evil?' So Satan answered the Lord and said, 'Does Job fear God for nothing? Have You not made a hedge around him, around his household, and around all that he has on every side? You have blessed the work of his hands, and his possessions have increased in the land. But now, stretch*

Who Is Responsible?

out Your hand and touch all that he has, and he will surely curse You to Your face!' And the Lord said to Satan, 'Behold, all that he has is in your power; only do not lay a hand on his person.' Then Satan went out from the presence of the Lord."

Job 1:6, "Now there was a day when the sons of God came to present themselves before the Lord, and Satan also came among them."

Let's get something *very* clear here, *the devil does not—**cannot**—present himself before God.* God hates satan because He hates evil. God and satan are enemies and are not having a dialogue with each other. God is seated in heaven, and satan is roaming the earth.

Ezekiel 28 and Isaiah 14 tell about how God threw Lucifer out of heaven. We see that the devil was called Lucifer and was the most beautiful angel in heaven. He was also the leader of all praise and worship that went on in heaven. *Then pride was found in him.* He rose up against God and tried to overthrow Him! Lucifer wanted to overtake heaven and control it. Can you imagine the huge amount of pride he must have had to have even begun to *think* of doing such a ridiculous thing?

After God threw him out of heaven, along with one third of the angels, they were cast to the earth and eternally banished from the presence of God. So, if the angels in heaven come before God, I can assure you there are no devils coming with them. Can you see the error in Job's opinion of spiritual things? Now, do not be too hard on Job; remember, he did not have a King James Bible or Christian TV and radio; he did not even have a good church to attend every Sunday! He was doing his best with the limited knowledge he had of God.

Can you see just how much satan must hate those of us who have chosen to live Christ-like? He hates us because we tell others about Jesus and how He came to forgive us of all our sin and made a way for us to be in right-standing with God. The devil can never be in that place again. He can never be forgiven because he had no tempter. He is the father of sin. That is why we are never to be in fellowship with him or those who follow him.

2 Corinthians 6:14-15, "Do not be unequally yoked together with unbelievers. For what fellowship has righteousness with lawlessness? And what communion has light with darkness?"

The devil is the embodiment of hate, lawlessness and darkness, and God is the embodiment of righteousness and light. There can be no fellowship or communion between them, which is why the angels and demons absolutely do not fellowship with each other in heaven or on earth. There are actually angels warring against the devil and his demons in the earth on our behalf.

> *Job 1:13-21, "Now there was a day when his sons and daughters were eating and drinking wine in their oldest brother's house; and a messenger came to Job and said, 'The oxen were plowing and the donkeys feeding beside them, when the Sabeans raided them and took them away—indeed they have killed the servants with the edge of the sword; and I alone have escaped to tell you!' While he was still speaking, another also came and said, 'The fire of God fell from heaven and burned up the sheep and the servants, and consumed them; and I alone have escaped to tell you!' While he was still speaking, another also came and said, 'The Chaldeans formed three bands, raided the camels and took them away, yes, and killed the servants with the edge of the sword; and I alone have escaped to tell you!' While he was still speaking, another also came and said, 'Your sons and daughters were eating and drinking wine in their oldest brother's house, and suddenly a great wind came from across the wilderness and struck the four corners of the house, and it fell on the young men, and they are dead; and I alone have escaped to tell you!' Then Job arose, tore his robe, and shaved his head; and he fell to the ground and worshiped. And he said; 'Naked I came from my mother's womb, and naked shall I return there. The Lord gave, and the Lord has taken away; blessed be the name of the Lord.'"*

Job did not understand how the spirit realm worked! This is quite understandable because in the Old Testament we find only eight references to the devil, whereas in the New Testament there are over one hundred and ten references. Back in Job's day they had a very limited and inaccurate understanding of who the devil was, as well as his position with God. The way Job understood it, the angels and demons were all somehow getting along with each other, and God and the devil worked together.

It is unfortunate that Christians in many churches today take Job 1:6 at face value. They do not look to see whether or not it lines up with the rest of the Bible. They figure that because it says it right there in the Bible, it must be the way it was! These people do not understand that it was *Job's* perception of the situation; it was not the truth about it. It was not what God did.

There is teaching in some circles that God and the devil are working together. It is believed that somehow satan is helping to punish people so they will turn to God. Believe me, *satan is **not** helping God get anybody saved!* God does not need the devil's help. He would never allow a vile reprobate like the devil to harm us in order to teach us something. The devil is working on his own; he is a free agent. He is out there trying to destroy people's lives and take as many to hell as he can. God and the devil are not sitting around making deals and talking about what they can do to us. Look what it says in Psalm 91:

> ***Psalm 91:1-16**, "He who dwells in the secret place of the Most High shall abide under the shadow of the Almighty. I will say of the Lord, 'He is my refuge and my fortress; My God, in Him I will trust.' Surely He shall deliver you from the snare of the fowler and from the perilous pestilence. He shall cover you with His feathers, and under His wings you shall take refuge; His truth shall be your shield and buckler. You shall not be afraid of the terror by night, nor of the arrow that flies by day, nor of the pestilence that walks in darkness, nor of the destruction that lays waste at noonday. A thousand may fall at your side and ten thousand at your right hand; but it shall not come near you. Only with your eyes shall you look, and see the reward of the wicked. Because you have made the Lord, who is my refuge, even the Most High, your habitation, no evil shall befall you, nor shall any plague come near your dwelling; for He shall give His angels charge over you, to keep you in all your ways. They shall bear you up in their hands, lest you dash your foot against a stone. You shall tread upon the lion and the cobra, the young lion and the serpent you shall trample underfoot. Because he has set his love upon Me, therefore I will deliver him; I will set him on high, because he has known My name. He shall call upon Me, and I will answer him; I will be with him in trouble; I will deliver him and honor him. With long life I will satisfy him, and show him My salvation."*

When we read what Jesus said about the devil in the New Testament we see who satan actually is and that he has absolutely no dealings with God. The devil is a vanquished foe!

Then Who Does Give Us Bad Things?

For years people have been looking at Job and saying, "Well, God will do that to you, you know. Poor old Job, he was such a wonderful guy. He was so righteous, and just *look* at what the Lord did to him! Look what God allowed Job to go through." They teach that God may do bad things to us in order to test us and teach us something. They have led us to believe that God causes the tragedy and problems in our lives. I have had it said to me so many times when a child, baby, or young person dies, "It must have been God's will. God knows best." There is no scriptural basis for those comments. Even pastors say those things at funerals. The Gospels show Jesus healing sick children and raising the dead.

Job was a religious man. Churches are full of religious people today, but how many of them really *know* the living, merciful, loving God that we serve? That is the vast difference between being "religious" and having a personal "relationship" with Jesus. Those who have a close, personal relationship with God have no doubt in their hearts and minds that God does not send us bad things to teach us something. They know this because they have read and accurately understood His whole Word.

Several years ago I conducted a funeral for a very wonderful Christian who had died tragically. I stated in my message that this death was not God's will and that He did not cause it. Yes, this individual is in heaven, but died out of time. I said that this is the work of the devil. Do you know that some of the religious people got very angry with me—even to the point that they went all over that city, telling people what I had said? They wanted to tar and feather me and run me out of town on a rail! Their religious doctrine taught them it was God who kills people so He can take them to heaven. I guess heaven must be pretty empty if God has to kill people to get them there. Look at what Jesus said:

> *John 10:10* (Amp), *"The thief comes only in order that he may steal and may kill and may destroy. I came that they may have and enjoy life, and have it in abundance—to the full, till it overflows."*

The thief here is *not* God; it is the devil. God has always wanted to save the people of the world, not destroy them. He desires for us to be conquerors and witnesses of His great love, might, and power. That is why we teach what the Word of God says—that all evil, sickness, and problems come from the devil, but all good things come from God. We teach that He only sends good our way. For instance, a good parent always seeks the greatest good for their children; they would never do anything to harm them. How much more would God the Father seek the greatest good for *His* children? Jesus said His desire was for us to enjoy life and have it in abundance, to the full—till it overflows. That does not sound to me like God is the one sending tragedy and trouble our way.

The devil is a bad spirit that is always seeking to do bad things in our lives. Our God is a good god who is always seeking to do good things in our lives. *We must learn the difference and stop being confused about this!*

We understand now that God is not out to "get" us. Job said, *"The Lord gave, and the Lord has taken away."* That is not true! The Lord does *not* give and then take it away. God is *not* schizophrenic! Wouldn't He be an awful god to be serving if that was the case? Picture it: You're doing real well. You've got a nice home, nice car, good paying job, a happy family life, growing closer and becoming more mature in God. But, there is always the thought in the back of your mind, "I wonder if God is going to take all this away from me." That would be a terrible way to go through life.

But that is how many people think. So when something goes bad in their lives, right away they think God is behind it. They do nothing about it, they take no authority over the situation, and they allow those good things to slide out of their lives. What they *should* do is what Jesus taught us to do.

> *Luke 10:19, "Behold, I give you the authority to trample on serpents and scorpions, and over all the power of the enemy, and nothing shall by any means hurt you."*

Several years ago, I was in South America holding meetings in some churches there. While I was there, a pastor in a neighboring village lost his wife to a lingering sickness. My pastor friend and I traveled to the village to attend the funeral of this woman. During the funeral the grieving husband (pastor) wanted to say a few words about his wife. He told what a good wife and mother she had always been. Those were good things to say, but then he turned against God, not deliberately but out of religious tradition.

He said that he did not know why God had taken his wife; he really loved her, and he and their children really needed her. "Oh, God, why did You take my wife?" he said with tears and great brokenness. All the people agreed that it was God who had done it.

If only he had known the truth! The thief (satan) killed her. Look what it says in Acts 10:

> *Acts 10:38, "How God anointed Jesus of Nazareth with the Holy Spirit and with power, who went about doing good and healing all who were oppressed by the devil, for God was with Him."*

Jesus came to save and heal, *not* to kill and steal our loved ones. Jesus came to give us a happy abundant life to enjoy to the full, to overflowing.

When this pastor was finished speaking, he said that he was taking some time off from the pastorate. He did not know if he would pastor again. He was angry and disappointed in God. How could he serve a God who killed his wife? How tragic that he had been taught wrong things about God! The devil was very successful in this attack. First, he took out a good Christian woman who was needed by many. Second, he caused such a great discouragement and confusion to her husband that he resigned as pastor. Who knows how many people will never come to know Jesus because this man was not there to share the love of Christ with them?

We have been given the power and authority to change our lives and those around us. We are *supposed* to exercise our power and authority over satan and situations in our lives that are not good. So, when bad things are happening to us, we need to get out of the mind-set that it is God's will, check to see if *we* are doing something that is opening doors of destruction, repent, and *take authority over the situation in the name of Jesus!*

Have you ever noticed that those people, who believe God "puts" sickness on them to teach them something, go to a doctor on a regular basis and receive medicine, shots, or some kind of treatment for that sickness or disease they believe God gave them? If they are doing that, they are actually in sin because now they are in rebellion toward God. If God really *has* given them sickness and disease to teach them something, then they ought to just take it, suffer with it, and learn whatever it is God is trying to teach them—not go to the doctor! These people believe God gave them the sickness to teach them something, but go to a doctor to try to get rid of it. I could never figure that one out!

We see in 1 Peter 2 that Jesus is our Healer.

> **1 Peter 2:24,** *"Who Himself bore our sins in His own body on the tree, that we, having died to sins, might live for righteousness—by whose stripes you were healed."*

We also need to realize that it is not *always* the devil that does things directly to us, either. A lot of times it is just our own mistakes, wrong choices, wrong opinions, refusal to change our mind-set on certain issues, or the absence of certain godly character traits operating in our lives. It seems that some people are just hell-bent on their own destruction—they charge through life like a bull in a china shop, determined to do things their own way, not caring what God has to say regarding the matter. Then they wonder why their life is in a crisis, and they expect God to fix it overnight!

The devil may very well have influenced these people's thoughts, but there are laws of nature as well as spiritual laws that take place when we do certain things. If we continue to drink, smoke, overeat, do drugs, drive recklessly, neglect the upkeep of our possessions or whatever it may be, one day the laws of nature will no doubt begin to manifest in our lives. The same goes for things we do in the spiritual realm.

We need to be assured that God did not send any evil thing into our lives in order to teach us something. For instance, He did not *cause* us to have that car accident to teach us not to speed. God is not in the destruction business. God probably tried a number of times to get us to slow down. But if we ignore His leading, He *will* let us go on our merry way and we will make our own mistakes, do dumb things, and God will still be there to help us out when we repent and ask for forgiveness.

The reason we like to blame God for everything bad that goes on in our lives is because there is usually no one responsible but ourselves. We do not like to take resonsibility for our mistakes; it must be someone else's fault. The devil may be the initiator of all evil and wickedness, but Jesus made a way to overcome it. In some cases we have no excuses and no one else to blame but ourselves. This is especially true of Christians who walk away from the Lord and into sin. They open themselves up to the works of the devil. *They* give him permission to destroy them. These people are backsliders and have walked away from their salvation; God will not go against their will. These people can, however, be saved if they repent and ask for forgiveness.

You have heard it said that people "fall" into sin. I want to set that straight. No one ever "falls" into sin—they make a conscious decision to walk after sin. Born again people can lose their salvation by walking away from the Lord and following sin again.

> *James 5:19-20,* "*Brethren, if anyone among you wanders from the truth, and someone turns him back, let him know that he who turns a sinner from the error of his way will save a soul from death and cover a multitude of sins.*"

Now, sometimes it *is* an out-and-out attack from the devil. This may happen often to those who are on fire for the things of God, living a holy and godly lifestyle, and are sharing Jesus with others. Lukewarm people who may call themselves Christians are attacked also because they have one foot in the world while trying to follow the Lord. The devil wants them to get discouraged, blame God, and follow him.

Do you realize that "satan" is not the devil's name? It *describes* who he is. The word satan means: the opponent, the hater, the accuser, the adversary. He resists and hinders whatever is good.

Has there ever been something good going on in your life—you are really growing in the Lord and seeing awesome things happen around you—then all of a sudden something comes against it? It is because the devil is hindering it, not God! In this situation, it is quite obvious that you are doing something powerful for the kingdom of God, and satan *hates* it!

If we know we are doing wrong and sinning, and the devil is attacking our lives, we have one choice—*repent!* We need to flee from the devil and run into the arms of Jesus. It is better to be attacked as an on-fire believer because there will be a reward for us in heaven. But if we are attacked as a lukewarm believer and walk away from our relationship with Jesus, there will be *no* reward and it could even lead us into eternal damnation.

God is for His children—always!

We need to get the revelation that God is *always for* us. If we are in business, working, trying to raise a family, going to church, seeking God, doing what we are supposed to be doing, but things are troubling us and hindering us—it is not God trying to show us something! God wants us to be successful in whatever we are doing as long as it is morally right and honest. God is going to help us to succeed. It is the devil, "satan," the hater, the spoiler, the one who hinders, who is going to try to stop the good things from happening in our lives.

One of the reasons satan tries so desperately to hinder success in Christians who are whole-heartedly living for God is because he knows that these Christians will use the money they earn to further the kingdom of God. More and more people all over the world will then hear about Jesus and what He did for them. Satan *hates* that kind of Christian! He usually does not take the time to bother nominal Christians too much. They open the doors for destruction themselves, and the devil obliges.

Thinking it is God's will to have illness is just plain ignorance and stupidity. That idea must stop in the body of Christ. Jesus is coming back for a pure people who are victorious. There may be areas in our lives that we still have not gotten victory over, but it does not mean that God *wants* us to remain in that condition. We need to continue speaking His Word over the situation. We are not to give up because the healing or deliverance we are believing for may manifest the very next time we speak out God's Word—*never quit!*

The body of Christ needs to get the revelation that God does *not* give us anything bad in order to teach us something. There are times when we simply cannot figure out why things are happening in our lives, but we *do* have a way of escape. By faith we keep confessing God's Word that pertains to the situation, believe He is able to watch over His Word to perform it, and do not doubt in our hearts that what we say we will have, then we *will* have it. Be of the mind-set that you will not blame God for anything, but that you will continually thank Him for the answer—and it *will* come!

Jesus is all we need. Staying surrendered to Jesus when we have asked Him to be Lord of our lives is essential. When we stay surrendered to Jesus, He will stay Lord of our lives!

CHAPTER THREE

"But I Am Righteous!"

Job 1:13-22, "Now there was a day when his sons and daughters were eating and drinking wine in their oldest brother's house; and a messenger came to Job and said, 'The oxen were plowing and the donkeys feeding beside them, when the Sabeans raided them and took them away—indeed they have killed the servants with the edge of the sword; and I alone have escaped to tell you!' While he was still speaking, another also came and said, 'The fire of God fell from heaven and burned up the sheep and the servants, and consumed them; and I alone have escaped to tell you!' While he was still speaking, another also came and said, 'The Chaldeans formed three bands, raided the camels and took them away, yes, and killed the servants with the edge of the sword; and I alone have escaped to tell you!' While he was still speaking, another also came and said, 'Your sons and daughters were eating and drinking wine in their oldest brother's house, and suddenly a great wind came from across the wilderness and struck the four corners of the house, and it fell on the young men, and they are dead; and I alone have escaped to tell you!' Then Job arose, tore his robe and shaved his head; and he fell to the ground and worshiped. And he said: 'Naked I came from my mother's womb, and naked shall I return there. The Lord gave, and the Lord has taken away; blessed be the name of the Lord.' In all this Job did not sin nor charge God with wrong."

Job 2:1-10, "Again there was a day when the sons of God came to present themselves before the Lord, and Satan came also among them to present himself before the Lord. And the Lord said to Satan, 'From where do you come?' So Satan answered the Lord and said, 'From going to and fro on the earth, and from walking back and forth on it.' Then the Lord said to Satan, 'Have you considered My servant Job, that there is none like him on the earth, a blameless and upright man, one who fears God and shuns evil? And still he holds fast to his integrity, although you incited Me against him, to destroy him without cause.' So Satan answered the Lord and said, 'Skin for skin! Yes, all that a man has he will give for his life. But stretch out Your hand now, and touch his bone and his flesh, and he will surely curse You to Your face!' And the Lord said to Satan, 'Behold, he is in your hand, but spare his life.' Then Satan went out from the presence of the Lord, and struck Job with painful boils from the sole of his foot to the crown of his head. And he took for himself a potsherd with which to scrape himself while he sat in the midst of the ashes. Then his wife said to him, 'Do you still hold fast to your integrity? Curse God and die!' But he said to her, 'You speak as one of the foolish women speaks. Shall we indeed accept good from God, and shall we not accept adversity?' In all this Job did not sin with his lips."

Job 2:11-13, *"Now when Job's three friends heard of all this adversity that had come upon him, each one came from his own place—Eliphaz the Temanite, Bildad the Shuhite, and Zophar the Naamathite. For they had made an appointment together to come and mourn with him, and to comfort him. And when they raised their eyes from afar, and did not recognize him, they lifted their voices and wept; and each one tore his robe and sprinkled dust on his head toward heaven. So they sat down with him on the ground seven days and seven nights, and no one spoke a word to him, for they saw that his grief was very great."*

Job 3:1-10, *"After this, Job opened his mouth and cursed the day of his birth. And Job spoke, and said: 'May the day perish on which I was born, and the night in which it was said, "A male child is conceived." May that day be darkness; may God above not seek it, nor the light shine upon it. May darkness and the shadow of death claim it; may a cloud settle on it; may the blackness of the day terrify it. As for the night, may darkness seize it; may it not rejoice among the days of the year, may it not come into the number of the months. Oh, may that night be barren! May no joyful shout come into it! May those curse it who curse the day, those who are ready to arouse the Leviathan. May the stars of its morning be dark; may it look for light, but have none, and not see the dawning of the day; because it did not shut up the doors of my mother's womb, nor hide sorrow from my eyes.'"*

Job 3:11-19, "'Why did I not die at birth? Why did I not perish when I came from the womb? Why did the knees receive me? Or why the breasts, that I should nurse? For now I would have lain still and been quiet, I would have been asleep; then I would have been at rest with kings and counselors of the earth. Who built ruins for themselves, or with princes who had gold, who filled their houses with silver; or why was I not hidden like a stillborn child, like infants who never saw light? There the wicked cease from troubling, and there the weary are at rest. There the prisoners rest together; they do not hear the voice of the oppressor. The small and great are there, and the servant is free from his master.'"

Job 3:20-26, "'Why is light given to him who is in misery, and life to the bitter of soul, who long for death, but it does not come, and search for it more than hidden treasures; who rejoice exceedingly, and are glad when they can find the grave? Why is light given to a man whose way is hidden, and whom God has hedged in? For my sighing comes before I eat, and my groanings pour out like water. For the thing I greatly feared has come upon me. And what I dreaded has happened to m e. I am not at ease, nor am I quiet; I have no rest, for trouble comes.'"

Self-righteousness is pride.

The agony of losing a loved one is extremely painful. If you have ever lost a spouse or child, then you can sympathize with Job. He lost all his children, his sheep and cattle, and his servants—all in one day! He was basically bankrupt and childless. It is very hard to fathom, but it did happen to Job.

In the natural, it would be difficult to trust God afterwards. Job, being a religious man and not knowing God personally, thought it was God allowing the devil to destroy him. If trouble should come, the one thing we should never do is blame God. God is not your problem!"

*Psalm 46:1, "God is our refuge and strength, **a very present help in trouble**."*

There can be many reasons why tragic things happen, but God is not one of them. Remember how Job perceived himself at the beginning of his book?

> *Job 1:1, "There was a man in the land of Uz, whose name was Job; and that man was blameless and upright, and one who feared God and shunned evil."*

This is how Job perceived himself. When he was talking to Eliphaz and the others that came to him, he kept defending himself, "I am such an upright man. I am such a righteous man." He never repented or tried to find out what was wrong with himself. He kept saying, "I am a righteous man."

We say that we are righteous because of Jesus Christ. We are not righteous because we are such wonderful people. We are not righteous because of the good things we do. We are righteous because of what Jesus did for us.

> *2 Corinthians 5:21, "For He made Him who knew no sin to be sin for us, that we might become the righteousness of God in Him."*

Job continued to explain what a righteous and upright man he was, and that he was blameless. He did not understand why God did these things to him, seeing how he was so religious and upright. Job really had a view of himself that was on the prideful side. He felt he was righteous of his own accord. This is one of the doors he opened to allow the devil to wreak havoc in his life—pride.

Know how the spirit realm works
In Job 1, we see *Job's* perception of how God and satan interact.

> *Job 1:11-12, "But now, stretch out Your hand and touch all that he has, and he will surely curse You to Your face!" And the Lord said to Satan, 'Behold, all that he has is in your power; only do not lay a hand on his person.' Then Satan went out from the presence of the Lord."*

We know now that God has absolutely no interaction with the devil. But I would like to point out what God said about Job, "Behold, all that he has is in your power." In the original Hebrew text the connotation was something like this, "Why do you trouble me? Job is already in your hands. He is already under your authority."

We know that once we received Jesus as our Lord and Savior, His authority was granted to us. This authority is ours to use over the devil and demons to set other captives free and bring people into the saving knowledge of Jesus Christ. This authority only works by faith in Christ, the Anointed One of God and His anointing. Let's take a look at a portion of Scripture found in Luke 10:

> *Luke 10:1, 8, 9, 17-19 (Amp), "Now after this the Lord chose and appointed seventy others and sent them out ahead of Him, two by two, into every town and place where He Himself was about to come (visit).*
>
> *Whenever you go into a town and they receive and accept and welcome you, eat what is set before you; And heal the sick in it and say to them, 'The kingdom of God has come close to you.'*
>
> *The seventy returned with joy, saying, Lord, even the demons are subject to us in Your name! And He said to them, I saw Satan falling like a lightning [flash] from heaven. Behold! I have given you authority and power to trample upon serpents and scorpions, and (physical and mental strength and ability) over all the power that the enemy [possesses]; and nothing shall in any way harm you."*

This account is regarding seventy men other than the twelve disciples. These seventy represent us. Look at verse 19 again. What Jesus gave them, He gives to us today; He gives this authority to those who will believe in Him.

Then Jesus says in **Luke 10:20** (Amp.), *"Nevertheless, do not rejoice at this, that the spirits are subject to you, but rejoice that your names are enrolled in heaven."* He is saying that we do not need to draw attention and rejoice because we have authority over the devil; that comes with the territory, so to speak, when we were born again. But we should rejoice because we are born of heaven and that is where our authority comes from.

The devil is the prince of the world. He is in charge of things down here. Until you were born again, you were under his dominion; you were in his hands, or in other words, you were under his authority.

Religous people, who do not have the knowledge of God, are living in pride if they think they are good enough to get to heaven by their own righteousness. Many people are actually in satan's hand. The only way to get out of his hand is to become born again. The blood of Jesus that was shed for us is the only thing that can get us out of the hand of the devil. When we made Jesus the Lord of our life, we entered into the sanctuary of God, and came under His protection and covering, and then we received the power of God to live free of satan.

Job's pride and self-righteousness opened the door for satan to come in. Job knew the devil had authority over him, but he thought it was God giving the devil that authority, not he himself. God did *not* give satan or his demons permission to oppress Job. *Job* gave satan permission through his religion and pride. He was in satan's hands already because he was not humble. Pride goes before a fall. Pride is sin.

God hates religion because religion is man's way to reach God. True Christianity is not a religion, but a relationship with our Redeemer, Jesus Christ. We reach God through faith. We get to know God by spending time with Him in Spirit and in truth—*not* through our intellect. Man has made Christianity into nothing more than a powerless religion.

> *John 8:31-32, "Then Jesus said to those Jews who believed Him, 'If you abide in My word, you are My disciples indeed. And you shall know the truth, and the truth shall make you free.'"*

We cannot abide in Christ unless we first repent of our sin nature and recognize Jesus as the only way to be forgiven and saved. Many of the Jews did just that during Jesus' earthly ministry.

Look at **John 8:33**, *"They answered Him, 'We are Abraham's descendants, and have never been in bondage to anyone. How can you say, "You will be made free"?'"* These were the religious Jews who trusted their religion. This same attitude of pride can be found in all churches today, even the ones that claim to be Full Gospel. Then Jesus showed them their error:

> *John 8:41-47, "'You do the deeds of your father.' Then they said to Him, 'We were not born of fornication; we have one Father—God.' Jesus said to them, 'If God were your Father, you would love Me, for I proceeded forth and came from God; nor have I come of Myself, but He sent Me. Why do you not understand My speech? Because you are not able to listen to My word. You are of your father the devil, and the desires of*

> *your father you want to do. He was a murderer from the beginning, and does not stand in the truth, because there is no truth in him. When he speaks a lie, he speaks from his own resources, for he is a liar and the father of it. But because I tell the truth, you do not believe Me. Which of you convicts Me of sin? And if I tell the truth, why do you not believe Me? He who is of God hears God's words; therefore you do not hear, because you are not of God.'"*

The truth from God's Word can really smack us where it hurts; but when we get smacked with it, we should come to our senses and ask Jesus to forgive us and help us turn from our error.

Humble Yourself Before God

1 Peter 5:6-8, "Therefore humble yourselves under the mighty hand of God, that He may exalt you in due time, casting all your care upon Him, for He cares for you. Be sober, be vigilant, because your adversary the devil walks about like a roaring lion, seeking whom he may devour."

Peter had an understanding of the subjects of pride and humility. He had a certain amount of pride in his character, but after humbling himself before God, he was exalted. God will do that in your life also. Get rid of the pride.

Some people ask *God* to keep them humble, but that is not what the Word says. The Word says that *we* are to humble ourselves, *then* God will exalt us "in due season." Humble yourself before God, and then patiently wait for Him to exalt you. It *will* happen because God said it would!

God does not want to humble us; He wants us to be humble by humbling ourselves. I learned this the hard way. God let me get to the end of myself. My rebellion toward God finally brought me to the place where I had nowhere to turn except to Jesus. When I surrendered and repented, He was right there to forgive me and receive me. He restored me and made something good out of my life. God is an awesome God, therefore, be humble. It is not about us; it is all about God.

Today the devil still uses that same attitude of pride that Job had when he put himself on a pedestal as being very righteous and upstanding before God. People who have pride open the door for the devil to enter.

In 1 Peter 5:8 there is a warning that reveals to us how satan operates. The devil is looking for areas of your life that are not surrendered to Jesus Christ because that is where he can get in and exploit the pride.

The people that I have seen fall away from God and get in trouble with the Lord are the people that have pride in their lives. They think they are so special and anointed that they ought to have a special ministry; otherwise nobody will see their exceptional gift. Those people fade away. They go off someplace looking for something to happen, where somebody will recognize their amazing gift. Usually these people do not have any real calling or gifting from God on their lives. They call themselves with their own soulish words.

I have been a Christian for over twenty-eight years, and I have found that it is usually the humble Christians who do not think they have anything much to offer the kingdom of God that God calls into places of five-fold ministry to the body of Christ. I have seen a number of Christians, including some ministers, open the door to the spirit of pride. They would start to think more highly of themselves than they should have and act superior to other believers.

Stay small in your own eyes.
Even if we are highly anointed and have many spiritual gifts, they are not ours. We did not create them and we cannot claim them as ours. Every good and precious gift comes from our Father in heaven. I have heard the Lord on several occasions say to me, "Stay small in your own eyes." The Lord has shown me that one of the main reasons most of those who we would call the "big name preachers" have become who they are is because they have remained small in their opinion of themselves. They know where promotion comes from and it is not from them.

> *Romans 12:3,* "For I say, through the grace given to me, to everyone who is among you, not to think of himself more highly than he ought to think, but to think soberly, as God has dealt to each one a measure of faith."

Reinhard Bonnke is an evangelist who God is using mightily because he is genuinely humble. When he first started ministering, he had a little office in Zambia. It cost $15 per month for rent, and he sent out Bible

"But I Am Righteous!"

correspondence courses to thousands of pastors throughout Africa. He was depending on financial support from Germany to help him out; however, one month he could not raise the $15 rent money. On the day that the rent was due, he went to the Post Office several times, hoping some money had arrived. Finally, the Post Office closed—still, no money to pay his rent.

As he was going home that night to his tiny house where his family was living, he cried out to God, saying that he could not even raise the money for rent or take care of his family properly. He questioned God about what he was doing there, and what good was he to Him! The Lord answered him saying that He would give him a million dollars for his faithfulness. Reverend Bonnke thanked the Lord for His promise and received it gratefully; but then he said, "Not just a million dollars, but give me a million souls, also!" The Lord said that he would have that, too.

He has faithfully served the Lord right where God placed him. He did not try to get in the lime light. Even today, as the world's greatest evangelist since Jesus, he tries to avoid the spot light. He humbly preaches the Word and relies on God and not his past successes. As far as I know Reverend Bonnke has seen over thirty million people come to the Lord! And that number continues to grow with each crusade he holds. He now sees one million people accept Jesus Christ as Lord in *one* crusade. Do you know why? Because he was humble. He did not walk around telling everyone about the great call on his life, nor did he grumble and complain about how nobody saw the wonderful gifts he had.

When I hear people murmuring and complaining that the pastor does not recognize their gift, bells, whistles, and red lights go off in my spirit man. Wrong spirit! That is the spirit of pride and arrogance—it is not the Spirit of God. You need to listen with your spirit and discernment when people are talking to you. Some can disguise their pride quite well for awhile, but eventually that spirit is exposed.

As Christians, we must be careful not to become haughty about anything good in our life because that opens doors that allow the devil to influence our thoughts and actions. If we are saved and doing mighty things for the kingdom of God, it is only because of His grace and power, not because of anything we did. It is what Jesus did for us.

CHAPTER FOUR

Fear Opens a Door

Fear Opens Doors into Your Life

Psalm 111:10, "The fear of the Lord is the beginning of wisdom…"

This kind of fear is the good kind of fear. It is speaking of a reverential awe and godly respect for the Most High God. We should never make light of God's power and sovereignty, neither are we to be so afraid of Him that we are unable to approach Him. We are to hold Him in the very highest esteem and honor, and come to Him with love, humility, and boldness. That kind of fear opens the door for wisdom and understanding to come into our lives.

However, there is another kind of fear that opens doors for the devil to come in.

Job 3:25, "For the thing I greatly feared has come upon me, and what I dreaded has happened to me."

There is a similar verse in Proverbs 23:

Proverbs 23:7, "For as he thinks in his heart, so is he."

This "thinking" is actually meditating on or dreaming about a thought. It can be a good thought or desire, or it can be a worrisome or evil thought. Whatever our thoughts dwell on we can receive—good or bad.

Job meditated on his fear, which was another open door allowing the devil to wreak havoc in his life. We see that Job had great fear that one day his children would die. That is why he would make sacrifices and pray all the time for them; he was afraid that they would sin, and then God would kill them. He was afraid that he would lose all his camels, donkeys, and cattle. He was in fear of losing his possessions and good name. He had a tremendous amount of faith in those fears, that one day they would indeed happen.

This is very common today. Wealthy people have a fear of losing all they have accumulated. Some of these people have a hard time sleeping because they are afraid the stock market will crash, and they will lose all their money while they are sleeping.

Along with pride, fear is another open door for the devil to get hold of your life. If we fear the wrong thing, it will harm us. We all have opportunities to slip into fear about something. Cast that thought down, immediately! The devil may try giving you thoughts and ideas of tragedy that could happen—get rid of it. That is not God. God does not put fear like that into you. God will warn you and show you things to pray against and intercept before they happen, but the warning is never accompanied by fearful dread. Job did not know all these things at that time.

Many people today live in fear. When a situation arises in their lives, when they hear of a new disease or whatever the case may be, they immediately open themselves up to fear and start listening to its voice. Yes, fear has a voice. We have all heard it many times in our lives. If we were to ask a person what their greatest fear was, they could give us a long list of things that speak to them.

There is another voice that wants to speak to us. It is called the voice of faith. This is the voice of God telling us He has the answers and He cares for us. The voice of fear originates with the devil. His voice is one of only lies. We have to train ourselves to hear the voice of faith. If we can hear fear speak, then we can hear faith speak too. But you cannot hear both at the same time. When we start meditating on God's Word, the voice of fear will be silenced and the voice of faith will speak loudly.

2 Corinthians 10:3-6, "For though we walk in the flesh, we do not war according to the flesh. For the weapons of our warfare are not carnal but mighty in God for pulling down strongholds, casting down arguments and every high thing that exalts itself against the knowledge of God, bringing every thought into captivity to the obedience of Christ, and being ready to punish all disobedience when your obedience is fulfilled."

Paul says that everything that exalts itself against God's Word is an enemy and that we must take it captive and cast it down. We must punish thoughts of fear with God's Word and our obedience to God.

Fear Is a Spirit

Fear is a spirit and it looks for a person who will receive it. If we listen to fear, it will control our thoughts and diminish our hope. It can totally debilitate us, bring us down, and defeat us. Its purpose is to keep us from being successful and being all that God intends for us to be. Fear is a choice. We must take authority over it, rebuke it, and forbid it to operate in our lives any longer.

Christians have a great help in time of trouble; their hope is in Jesus Christ, and no matter what the situation is they can trust Jesus to deliver them. God's Word is full of hope and His promises. The Psalms are an especially powerful encouragement. Here are just a few verses telling us of God's love and protection for His people:

Psalm 28:6-9, "Blessed be the Lord, because He has heard the voice of my supplications! The Lord is my strength and my shield; my heart trusted in Him, and I am helped; therefore my heart greatly rejoices, and with my song I will praise Him. The Lord is their strength, and He is the saving refuge of His anointed. Save Your people, and bless Your inheritance; shepherd them also, and bear them up forever."

Psalm 31:3-5, "For You are my rock and my fortress; therefore, for Your name's sake, lead me and guide me. Pull me out of the net which they have secretly laid for me, for You are my strength. Into Your hand I commit my spirit; You have redeemed me, O Lord God of truth."

Fear Opens a Door

Psalm 31:19, "Oh, how great is Your goodness, which You have laid up for those who fear You, which You have prepared for those who trust in You in the presence of the sons of men!"

Psalm 34:7-8, "The angel of the Lord encamps all around those who fear Him, and delivers them. Oh, taste and see that the Lord is good; blessed is the man who trusts in Him!"

The fear we see in these verses is the reverence, respect, and love we have for God. This fear brings hope, relief, peace, and happiness in our lives.

If you wholeheartedly believe God's Word, then it will not be possible to believe fear. You cannot operate in both at the same time. Fear is of the devil while hope, trust, and faith are from the Lord. Our faith is what God uses to get His blessings and promises into our lives; in the same respect, our fear is what the devil uses to bring havoc into our lives. Psalm 91 says it so well:

Psalm 91:1-16, "He who dwells in the secret place of the Most High shall abide under the shadow of the Almighty. I will say of the Lord, 'He is my refuge and my fortress; my God, in Him I will trust.' Surely He shall deliver you from the snare of the fowler and from the perilous pestilence. He shall cover you with His feathers, and under His wings you shall take refuge; His truth shall be your shield and buckler. You shall not be afraid of the terror by night, nor of the arrow that flies by day, nor of the pestilence that walks in darkness, nor of the destruction that lays waste at noonday. A thousand may fall at your side, and ten thousand at your right hand; but it shall not come near you. Only with your eyes shall you look, and see the reward of the wicked. Because you have made the Lord, who is my refuge, even the Most High, your dwelling place, no evil shall befall you, nor shall any plague come near your dwelling; for He shall give His angels charge over you, to keep you in all your ways. In their hands they shall bear you up, lest you dash your foot against a stone. You shall tread upon the lion and the cobra, the young lion and the serpent you shall trample underfoot. Because he has set his love upon Me, therefore I will deliver him; I will set him on high, because he has known My name. He shall call upon Me, and I will answer him; I will be with him in trouble; I will deliver him and honor him. With long life I will satisfy him, and show him My salvation."

God is our help and Deliverer. If we would only set *all* our love, heart, mind, and strength in Him, we would see His awesome power at work in our lives.

Watch What You Say

People oftentimes live in such fear of a certain thing happening to them that eventually it *does* happen. It happens because they are continually speaking out that fear; they have a great deal of faith that what they are in fear of *will* happen. Fear is an open door for satan to wreak havoc in your life. Many people have more belief in their fears and doubts than they do in the Word of God. So when the thing they feared most does happen, they say, "See? I just *knew* it was going to happen!"

When faith in God is operating in a person, he or she speaks His Word, trusting wholeheartedly in the Lord. But when fear operates in a person's life, the words they speak will show that fear. Your words will either deliver you or ensnare you. *Watch your words!*

The words of Job's mouth in Job 3:25 were his snare. He feared that bad things were going to happen. He feared that destruction and problems were going to come upon his household. That is exactly what happened. He ensnared himself with fear and he spoke it out.

2 Timothy 1:7, "For God has not given us a spirit of fear, but of power and of love and of a sound mind."

People who have a relationship with the living God do not have fear. They live by faith in God, believing His whole Word.

1 John 4:8, "He who does not love does not know God, for God is love."

1 John 4:18, "There is no fear in love; but perfect love casts out fear, because fear involves torment. But he who fears has not been made perfect in love.

I talked to a full gospel, Spirit-filled preacher a few years back. We were talking about healing, and he did not have a lot of faith in that area. He said to me, "What about Job? God made Job sick, didn't He?" I asked him where he had gone to Bible school. He had been a preacher for over twenty-five years and still thought it was a blessing to be like Job, as if God did all those things to him. He thought sickness was of God. With this kind of mentality about God, it is no wonder people have fear in their lives. These people see God and the devil on the same level. If people believe that God is the destroyer and brings problems in their life, they will have an open door to fear. The devil may be our problem and our mouths may be our problem, *but God is not our problem!* This well-meaning pastor experienced many tragedies in his life and ministry; he also suffered with much sickness. it is not enough to be well meaning; you must have faith and resist fear.

Do not give the devil any opportunity to ruin your life by accepting thoughts of fear. If they try to come on you, it is best to follow Jesus' example: "It is written …"

CHAPTER FIVE

Accused Falsely

Recognize the Enemy

Job falsely accused God at least seventy-four times. The first one is found in Job 1:

> ***Job 1:21***, *"And he said: 'Naked I came from my mother's womb, and naked shall I return there. The Lord gave, and the Lord has taken away; blessed be the name of the Lord.'"*

There is no other Scripture that agrees with this statement. My Bible says that God wants to bless us. He does not give us good things and then take them away. He does not destroy our families and property. If this has happened to you, it was from something other than God!

Proverbs says that our words ensnare us:

> ***Proverbs 6:2***, *"You are snared by the words of your mouth; you are taken by the words of your mouth."*

What we say can bring trouble into our lives. As we know, the Lord gives us good things, but He does not take them away. Job made a false accusation against God. It was the devil who took Job's goods away because of the "open doors" in his character, which gave the devil access to mess with him.

We need to recognize our enemy. Job would have done well to have known who his enemy was. As we know, his enemy was the devil, not God. Job talked about the devil coming and asking for him, and still he put the blame on God. He never blamed the devil; it was always God.

Some people are like that today. They seem to think that God caused their little child to die because He wanted them in heaven to be with Him. Where *do* they get that from? I believe they get it from man's reasoning and bad religion—*not* from God's Word. Although this was Job's opinion of God, that does not make it right. I would not build my doctrine about God on the book of Job. Job did not even *know* God. (I will show this in a later chapter.)

I had a lady tell me how God had taken her child through a tragic accident, and she was giving God all the credit for her child's death. I said, "It wasn't God who killed your baby; it was the work of the devil." I was almost stunned when she looked at me like I was an alien from outer space. She said, "Why would the devil do that?" I quickly answered, *"Because he hates every living person on the face of the earth, and he wants everyone dead!"*

He does not want God's crowning creation—man—to worship and follow God. The devil hates God and everyone who loves Him. The devil is nothing more than a fallen angel. He was once a beautiful cherub who worshipped God, but he rebelled, and God threw him and the other rebellious angels out of heaven—never to return.

Now *we* are the new worshipers of God, and we have fellowship and relationship with the Most High God. The devil hates us because we stand in his former place, the place he can never return to. We are going to heaven to be with God for all eternity, and the devil is going to hell for all eternity, to be punished with hellfire.

> ***John 10:10 (Amp),*** *"The thief comes only in order to steal and kill and destroy. I came that they may have and enjoy life, and have it in abundance (to the full, till it overflows)."*

Jesus calls satan the thief who causes all the evil in the world. Jesus said that He gives overflowing and abundant life, which includes life here on earth as well as in heaven!

In the second chapter of Job, the devil supposedly came back and asked for Job himself. When Job falsely accused God of taking away his livelihood, he opened up another door for the devil to enter his life and wreak havoc. God, in His mercy, actually did spare Job's life, but everything else was ruined.

Job's False Accusations

I have already shared Job's false accusation found in Job 1:21. Now I would like to share with you some of the other false charges Job made against God.

> *Job 7:14, "Then You scare me with dreams and terrify me with visions."*

Does God give us bad dreams, nightmares, and tormenting thoughts? No, that is the work of the devil.

> *Job 9:17-18, "For He crushes me with a tempest and multiplies my wounds without cause. He will not allow me to catch my breath, but fills me with bitterness."*

That is most definitely not the loving God we know! That is the devil's devices.

These are charges that Job made against God. The devil's work includes getting us to blame God, and to not blame him. His work is to get us to point our finger at God and say, "God, why did you do this to me? God, You are my problem; You allowed this to happen."

We ought to recognize the devil is a liar, and *he* is the one causing the problems. We do not need to go on and on about all that he does because that would be giving him glory. We simply need to put him in his place, under our feet, and *keep him there!* According to Luke 10:19, we ought to point a finger at the guilty party and tell him to be gone in Jesus' name!

> *Luke 10:19, "Behold, I give you the authority to trample on serpents and scorpions, and over all the power of the enemy, and nothing shall by any means hurt you."*

Accused Falsely

I remember one very exciting Father's Day. My children were at our home having a wonderful time and honoring me. Then my daughter and her husband announced they were expecting a baby. We were all surprised and very blessed. The rest of our time together that day was spent talking about the new baby. Names were discussed for a boy and for a girl, and we were making lots of plans for this new child. There is nothing as exciting as a new baby coming into the world.

However, this joy soon turned to sorrow for our family. Within a few short weeks, at my daughter's routine doctor's exam, they discovered the baby was no longer living. I still remember the phone call and all the pain that my daughter and her husband went through. It was a shock for us and no one could understand how this could have happened.

Melanie and her husband, David, are two of the finest Christians I know. I do not say this because they are my children. I say it because it is true. I know they live pure and holy lives with no smoking, drinking, or sin. They live consecrated lives to God.

Melanie is the worship leader in our church, and David serves in many capacities. He keeps things flowing smoothly for us. It was very difficult for my wife, Dawn, and me to watch as they went through this ordeal and walked it out before God. These two people make Dawn and me very proud of them.

Not once did they blame God for this loss. Not once did they feel it was a test from God. There was no anger or bitterness toward God. They both know the Word and what a good God we serve. None of us could explain what happened, neither could the doctor, but God has healed them and poured out His love on them.

In times like this you find out what you believe and if you have faith. They continued to serve God in the church and be an example to everyone. We are called to be living epistles. Our lives should emulate the love of Christ.

The good news is that fifteen months later they gave birth to a beautiful, completely healthy baby girl! They named her Victoria, which is the feminine form of the word Victory.

What the devil meant for tragedy, God turned for good. No matter what happens or how bleak a situation may look, God is not your problem. He is your Deliverer!

More False Accusations

> *Job 9:23-24, "If the scourge slays suddenly, He laughs at the plight of the innocent. The earth is given into the hand of the wicked. He covers the faces of its judges. If it is not He, who else could it be?"*

> *Job 10:3, "Does it seem good to You that You should oppress, that You should despise the work of Your hands, and smile on the counsel of the wicked?"*

> *Job 10:16, "If my head is exalted, You hunt me like a fierce lion, and again You show Yourself awesome against me."*

> *Job 16:7, "But now He has worn me out; You have made desolate all my company."*

> *Job 16:14, "He breaks me with wound upon wound; He runs at me like a warrior."*

These are terrible things to say about God. Job was putting the blame on the wrong one. Let's continue on in the book of Job and see why he thought that way.

In Job 30, he continued talking about God and was still defending himself because he did not know why all this had happened to him:

> *Job 30:11-12, "Because He has loosed my bowstring and afflicted me, they have cast off restraint before me. At my right hand the rabble arises; they push away my feet, and they raise against me their ways of destruction."*

What Job was saying here was that God had afflicted him and made him weak; that there was nothing he could do. These were the words of a religious man who did not know the God of love or have a relationship with Him.

> *Job 30:20-23, "I cry out to You, but You do not answer me; I stand up, and You regard me. But You have become cruel to me; with the strength*

> *of Your hand You oppose me. You lift me up to the wind and cause me to ride on it; You spoil my success. For I know that You will bring me to death, and to the house appointed for all living."*

Here Job called God cruel and said that He had spoiled his success. Those are terrible things to say about God, yet he continued to say that he was a righteous and pure man. Job simply did not realize that it was the devil messing up his life because of the doors he had opened. Job had no clue about the love of God. He could praise God in the good times, but he cursed Him in the bad times. This is what the devil wants us to do, curse God when things are going wrong—*do not do it!*

These are just a few of Job's false accusations; it gets worse as he goes on. Please do not think that I am saying that Job was a bad person. He was a good man and loved his children. He also loved God, but had a wrong perception of who He was. Job also lacked the understanding he needed to overcome the devil. Many Christians today have these same misconceptions about God. They miss out on the great things God has in store for them.

> ***John 10:10(Amp)**, "The thief comes only in order to steal and kill and destroy. I came that they may have and enjoy life, and have it in abundance (to the full, till it overflows)."*

Job knew about God, but he did not know God.
Job knew something about God. He was taught something, but he did not communicate directly with the Lord. Abraham, Jacob, Joseph, and Moses all communicated directly with God. These men *knew* God, so it was possible for Job to commune with God; however, at this point in his life he did not do so.

The same holds true for many today. Many people have a form of religion, but not a close relationship with God. That is how I was before I became born again. For instance, when I was seventeen years old, I liked to write stories and poetry. The Holy Ghost brought one of the poems I had written before I was saved to my memory:

> Old men sitting in the park
> Feeding the pigeons
> Thinking about the world gone by
> Young men losing their lives in the war
> Where is God?
> Is He out to lunch?

I wrote this poem in 1968. The Vietnam War was raging; I was a hippie and peace activist, and the poem was voicing my opinion of God. *Why is God doing this?* I thought. *Why is He letting all these young men die over there in Vietnam? Has God gone on vacation or something? Why doesn't God do something?*

The Lord then said to me, "That is just the way Job looked at things, like *I* was the problem, like *I* was the one doing all those evil things." He has taught me that the reason we have conflict, fighting, and war is because of the work of the devil and sin. The righteous have a God-given right to fight back and defend themselves, their families, and their country.

> ***James 3:16****, "For where envy and self-seeking exist, confusion and every evil thing are there."*

The Holy Ghost pointed out to me that my attitude toward Him was very similar to Job's—I had known about God, I was searching for God, but I did not *know* Him. I finally knew God when I was thirty-one years old. That was when I became born again. That was when I came to *know* God and have a personal relationship with Him. Before that I only had a form of religion, like Job had. It is not enough to believe that God exists—even the demons believe that—we must know God personally and intimately.

So, do not let anyone convince you that God is putting you through things just so you can learn something from them and get closer to Him. God is bigger than that; He does not need help from the devil to teach you something or help you to have a closer relationship with Him.

> ***1 Timothy 6:3-4****, "If anyone teaches otherwise and does not consent to wholesome words, even the words of our Lord Jesus Christ, and to the doctrine which accords with godliness, he is proud, knowing nothing, but*

is obsessed with disputes and arguments over words, from which come envy, strife, reviling, evil suspicions…"

Once I was born again, I realized it was not God, but rather the devil, that caused the Vietnam War and killed all those young men over there. It was God who *ended* it! There are still wars today, and God is not causing them. The devil is out there spreading his hate and lies, which will eventually cause a great deal of strife, discord, hatred, and war.

The spirit of Islam is causing almost every war and all the terrorism we are seeing today. I have met many Muslims, and they are nice people who are caught up in a false religion that is *not* a love and peace religion; it is a religion of intolerance, hatred, and revenge. This large, false religion will bring the world to Armageddon. Then all the nations will weep and wail when they see Jesus, the Son of God, descend from heaven and stand on the temple mount, and there will be no mosque there!

CHAPTER SIX

Grace, Mercy, and Judgment

The Dialogue

There is a dialogue between Job and his friends that went on for days. The first seven days they just sat there in astonishment about what had happened to Job. Eventually they began a thirty-five chapter discourse as to why all this happened to Job. One friend would speak and then Job would defend himself. They all had a different angle that they were coming from. I encourage you to read the complete book of Job for the full impact.

Eliphaz the Temanite
Job 4 and 5

Eliphaz believed that Job was being punished for some evil that he did not know about. He believed that it was something that Job did not remember doing and that he needed to search his heart so God would reveal it to him. Then God would forgive him and prosper him again after he repented. Wouldn't it be awful if that were actually the case? Just imagine if it were you. Any time you happen to do a little something wrong, everything you have is wiped out and your body gets full of sores—all this so you can *learn* something. Such horrible destruction would not come on your life for something that minuscule.

The biggest error here is blaming God for Job's problems. This is a Hindu belief called *karma*. When something bad happens, they believe that one of their 360 million gods is punishing them.

Grace, Mercy, and Judgment

Eliphaz did not know God either and, like Job, had his own confused ideas about God. He was not very comforting to Job, to say the least. We must be careful not to speak of things we don't understand.

> *Job 6:1, "Then Job answered and said: 'Oh, that my grief were fully weighed, and my calamity laid with it on the scales! For then it would be heavier than the sand of the sea—therefore my words have been rash.'"*

Now Job answers Eliphaz. Job knows he has been unjustly judged. In the sixth chapter of Job, we see a few of Job's statements in defense of his deplorable situation:

> *Job 6:4, "For the arrows of the Almighty are within me; my spirit drinks in their poison; the terrors of God are arrayed against me."*

Job continued to explain his situation by blaming God. This is never a good thing to do because God is not your problem.

> *Job 6:8-10, "Oh, that I might have my request, that God would grant me the thing that I long for! That it would please God to crush me, that He would loose His hand and cut me off! Then I would still have comfort; though in anguish I would exult, He will not spare; for I have not concealed the words of the Holy One."*

Job feels it would be better to be dead than to go through this great difficulty. He also believes that it would actually please God to kill him. If you have ever gone through an unbearable time that seemed like it would never end, you might have thought that God was trying to kill you, that He did not care about you or even know that you existed. In reality, God was waiting for you to stop blaming Him and start putting your trust in Him. He was waiting for you to see Him as your Deliverer.

> *1 Peter 4:12-15, "Beloved, do not think it strange concerning the fiery trial which is to try you, as though some strange thing happened to you; but rejoice to the extent that you partake of Christ's sufferings, that when His glory is revealed, you may also be glad with exceeding joy. If you are reproached for the name of Christ, blessed are you, for the Spirit of glory and of God rests upon you. On their part He is blasphemed, but on your part He is glorified. But let none of you suffer as a murderer, a thief, and evildoer, or as a busybody in other people's matters."*

Many believers will go through trials that they cannot explain or understand. If we keep our eyes on the Lord, trust Him, and realize He is not causing us to suffer, we will grow and learn from life's trials and difficult situations.

1 Peter 5:7, "Casting all your care upon Him, for He cares for you."

If God was causing your problems, then He would not say for you to cast them upon Him. He would tell you to bear them yourself until you have learned your lesson.

1 Peter 5:8, "Be sober, be vigilant; because your adversary the devil walks about like a roaring lion, seeking whom he may devour."

In this Scripture, we are told to have control over our lives and to be watchful because the devil goes about hunting the weak Christian; the one who does not know the Word is still dabbling in the world and is being led by the flesh and his or her own will. Here Peter is telling us that trials will come, but they are not from God.

The *devil* is your problem, and he does not want you to know that he is your problem. He does not reveal himself. He is a sly thing; he deceives people into thinking that God is their problem and is doing all these cruel, mean things to them. The devil has many pastors preaching it. They will say things like, "You just never know what God is going to put you through."

I have started several churches over the years and have put pastors in them. Each time there were attacks against them. I knew God was not trying to close the church that He told me to start. If He wanted it closed, He would have spoken to me about it. Each time I knew it was the work of the devil. As I kept my faith in God, He empowered and anointed me to defeat the devil.

When I pioneered the church I pastor today, I experienced a horrendous attack of the devil. I saw how he can deceive believers when they are not in control of their thoughts or watchful of his devices. I had two men who became prideful and opened the door to the devil. They decided they would steal the successful church that God had called, anointed, and appointed me to start. They went so far as to try to steal the physical building and its contents by changing the locks on all the doors. Then they threatened me and said they would hurt me and my family if we did not leave town and give them the church. This was like the mafia operating. They were so deceived, and they could not even see it. There was no reasoning with them. Their minds had been taken over by the devil.

I did not blame God for all this trouble. I put my trust in Him and watched how He delivered the building back to me, along with most of the congregation still intact. That was in 1999. Today this church is moving and shaking in our region, and has become an international mission force in the earth. I now take teams to foreign countries and preach to thousands and tens of thousands. Many come to Christ and get healed and delivered from the oppression of the devil. Had I blamed God for my church troubles or thought that God was trying to teach me something, I could have lost the whole church. I would have hindered God from delivering me.

Based on what he says in Job 6, Job is very hurt by his friend's words:

> *Job 6:14-15, "To him who is afflicted, kindness should be shown by his friend, even though he forsakes the fear of the Almighty. My brothers have dealt deceitfully like a brook, like the streams of the brooks that pass away."*

Then Job continues to blame God:

> *Job 7:5, "My flesh is caked with worms and dust, my skin is cracked and breaks out afresh."*

> *Job 7:11, "Therefore I will not restrain my mouth; I will speak in the anguish of my spirit; I will complain in the bitterness of my soul."*

> *Job 7:20-21, "Have I sinned? What have I done to You, O watcher of men? Why have You set me as Your target, so that I am a burden to myself? Why then do You not pardon my transgression, and take away my iniquity? For now I will lie down in the dust, and You will seek me diligently, but I will no longer be."*

Bildad the Shuhite
Job 8

Job 8:1-6, "Then Bildad the Shuhite answered and said: 'How long will you speak these things, and the words of your mouth be like a strong wind? Does God subvert judgment? Or does the Almighty pervert justice? If your sons have sinned against Him, He has cast them away for their transgression. If you would earnestly seek God and make your supplication to the Almighty, if you were pure and upright, surely now He would awake for you, and prosper your rightful dwelling place.'"

Bildad the Shuhite turned to the idea of tradition and suggested that Job was a hypocrite. He said that Job must have sinned in order for him to have so much trouble and disaster. He said that Job ought to repent for his sin, because this was God's judgment on him.

Job 9:21-22, "I am blameless, yet I do not know myself; I despise my life. It is all one thing; therefore I say, 'He destroys the blameless and the wicked.'"

Here Job is still trying to defend himself as being righteous, but in order to be righteous, your lifestyle must convey integrity and justice. If those traits were present, he would not blame God. Job may have been a good father, husband, herdsman, employer, and he may have even been religious, but these things do not make one righteous. Our integrity and justice have to be in line with God and His will.

In Numbers 15:32-36, there is an account of the man who broke the law of the Sabbath by picking up sticks. God's law forbade the people from doing any work on the Sabbath. The people brought this man to Moses to be judged. Moses inquired of the Lord, and the Lord said that he must be stoned for his sin.

In my mind, living under the grace of Jesus Christ, that seemed harsh. For several days after I read this it would come to my remembrance, and on one occasion the Lord spoke to me and asked me a question. He said, "Was stoning that man just or unjust?" I quickly answered back, "It was just, God, because it was Your law." I am always in agreement with God, His Word, and His will. To disagree with God is unrighteous and is sin.

Job continues to lay the blame on God:

> *Job 10:2-3*, *"I will say to God, 'Do not condemn me; show me why You contend with me. Does it seem good to You that You should oppress, that You should despise the work of Your hands, and smile on the counsel of the wicked?'"*

> *Job 10:7-8*, *"… although You know that I am not wicked, and there is no one who can deliver from Your hand? Your hands have made me and fashioned me, an intricate unity; yet You would destroy me."*

Zophar the Naamathite
Job 11

Zophar the Naamathite condemned Job and told him that he was a sinner and was actually getting less than what he deserved. He said that Job should repent as well. He based his remarks on that day's theology, which was that if something bad was happening to you it was God doing it to you because there was sin in your life.

> *Job 11:3-5*, *"Should your empty talk make men hold their peace? And when you mock, should no one rebuke you? For you have said, 'My doctrine is pure, and I am clean in your eyes.' But oh, that God would speak, and open His lips against you …"*

> *Job 11:14-15*, *"If iniquity were in your hand, and you put it far away, and would not let wickedness dwell in your tents; then surely you could lift up your face without spot; yes, you could be steadfast, and not fear."*

I am not making light of sin, for sin will indeed affect our relationship with our heavenly Father. It will cause negative results and even sickness and eventual death, if we refuse to repent and ask forgiveness.

Job continues to defend himself and answers many things in Chapter 12, but in verse 6 he says:

> *Job 12:6*, *"The tents of robbers prosper, and those who provoke God are secure—in what God provides by His hand."*

Job was *definitely* lacking knowledge of God. And then he prays a pitiful prayer:

> *Job 13:20-22, "Only two things do not do to me, then I will not hide myself from You: Withdraw Your hand far form me, and let not the dread of You make me afraid. Then call, and I will answer; or let me speak, then You respond to me."*

I now know why God told me to write this book: *For too many years pastors have been preaching "Poor old Job, look what God did to him. You just never know what God is trying to teach you."* The Lord spoke to me and said that this is blasphemy. It is a misrepresentation of His character. In other words, God hates that teaching, and it is a stench in His nostrils. It stinks to high heavens, and the church must stop it.

God is not your problem; the devil is. God did not give the devil permission to trouble your life. You did—by your words, attitude, and wrong doctrine. God was not Job's problem either; the devil was. God did not give him permission to do all those horrible things to Job. Job did—by his words, attitude, and wrong doctrine.

What Friends!

Those were his "friends!" Here Job was, going through something horrible, and they felt that God had done this to him and was punishing him. Through all this discourse with these three men, Job maintained his self-righteousness and that he was pure in heart. He never backed down. He believed that he was a righteous man, upright before God, and that he had done no wrong. He based that on his theology that *if* he did enough *good* works, God would love him and wouldn't do anything bad to him.

Job was confused as to why all those things had happened to him. He did not understand that it was actually his pride and fear that opened the door for the devil to come in and wreak havoc in his life. Pride and fear are the devil's brothers. We give the devil control of our lives when we allow these two ungodly spirits to operate.

We had some friends from India a long time ago who had been raised as

Hindus, and they explained what karma is in that religion. If they happened to bang a knee against the coffee table, cut a finger, develop a wart, or anything not good, it was because the gods were punishing them for something bad they had done. That is karma. They live their whole life thinking that all little bruises or bad things that happen to them are because they did something bad. They believe that they are getting their punishment here on earth, and they are doing penance all the time because the gods are punishing them as they go through life. And, hopefully, they will not make too many mistakes, so that when they die, they will come back in a higher order.

There are some Christians who believe something along that line, too. They try to do good works and kind acts to appease God. They go through religious acts and make sacrifices, hoping to be right with Him.

It says in Ephesians 2 that Jesus came from heaven to save us; it was the free gift of grace from our heavenly Father:

> ***Ephesians 2:8-9***, *"For by grace you have been saved through faith, and that not of yourselves; it is the gift of God, not of works, lest anyone should boast."*

If we do good works, we must give all the glory to Jesus. Our heavenly Father sent Him to die in our place and pay the debt for our sins, sins which He never even committed. No one can earn salvation, but we *can* receive it by faith in Jesus Christ.

We have to be very careful not to point an accusing finger at anyone when something bad happens in their life. Be careful! Sometimes there are even people that have done bad things to you in the past, and you may see something happen to them; never say, "See? There's his judgment!" I know that God *will* judge people and deal with them, but we do not want to be in a place where we set ourselves up as judge. We do not want to judge everybody's life and everything that is happening to them. That is God's business, not ours. Our place is to forgive those who trespass against us and walk in love toward them. It may not seem easy. Our flesh will not like it, but it is the Word of God. We are required to obey God, and then we will have peace and joy in our lives.

*Matthew 6:9-12, "In this manner, therefore, pray: Our Father in heaven, hallowed be Your name. Your kingdom come. Your will be done on earth as it is in heaven. Give us this day our daily bread. **And forgive us our debts, as we forgive our debtors**"* (emphasis added).

Mark 11:25, "And whenever you stand praying, if you have anything against anyone, forgive him, that your Father in heaven may also forgive you."

When bad things do happen to people, do not tell others about it. Simply pray for the situation and do not wish evil or bad on *anybody*. I do not care what has been done to you; do not even think in your heart that God would "get" them. We should be thinking, "God get *to* them!" That is what they need, *not* our accusations and judgments. Then we need to watch our own attitude, because there is not one of us who is perfect and above reproach. We all have made mistakes.

What we do is not what Christianity should be based on. Christianity is based on grace and the work that *Jesus* did for us at the cross. We have to always keep in mind that God is *for* us and *with* us; He is not out to "get" us. God always desires the best in our lives. We have to remember that so when things are not going right we are not thinking, "Oh, God, why are You doing this to me? Why are you letting this happen to me?"

Whose Fault Is It?

God is not necessarily letting bad things happen to us. A lot of times it is *we* who are letting things happen to us because of what we have done or said. It may have been out of fear or pride, or because we have not kept order in our lives and homes, that things are now happening. It may have nothing to do with the devil; it may be our own inadequacies and mistakes, such as rebelling and not obeying God's Word.

God, in His mercy, will help you get through those situations. There is a difference between grace and mercy: **Grace** is God giving you things that you really do not deserve; **Mercy** is God *not* giving you what you really *do* deserve! We should be just as grateful for God's mercy as we are for His grace.

Grace, Mercy, and Judgment

We should thank God that He is not the kind of god that sticks His finger in our face and says, "Well, you should have known better. You should have been reading your Bible and figured it out." *We* are like that, but God is not. He will simply encourage us to come to Him and to start over. He will show us what we need to start doing or stop doing; He will show us how we need to change in order to get our life back on *His* track.

Keep in mind that there is a time and place for correction and advice, but usually it comes from the pastor to whom the individual is submitted. If something bad is going on in someone's life—pray for them! Encourage them to draw closer to God than they ever have before and *do not judge them*.

CHAPTER SEVEN

The Mouthpiece of God

Elihu, the Youngest Friend

For 25 chapters Job's friends gave their opinions of his situation. They tried to figure out what was wrong or what he had done. In every chapter they would judge him and he would say that it was not true because he had done this or that. Job continued to blame God.

Eliphaz, Bildad, and Zophar accused Job of being wicked. They were trying to find an answer to Job's disasters in their own reasoning; but Job continued to defend himself and to blame God.

In Job 32, his friends finally gave up on him.

> *Job 32:1, "So these three men ceased answering Job, because he was righteous in his own eyes."*

They could not get through to Job because he was righteous in his own eyes and was not going to budge from that. He took no responsibility for his troubles. It was somehow all God's fault. Job thought that God was responsible for his miserable condition.

In Job 32, we meet the fourth friend, Elihu. He was the only one that had any wisdom. I like Elihu. We ought to want to be like him and not the other three. We should desire the wisdom of God, *not* man's wisdom.

Jams 1:5, *"If any of you lacks wisdom, let him ask of God, who gives to all liberally and without reproach, and it will be given to him."*

Now let's see what Elihu says of Job and his situation:

Job 32:2-22, *"Then the wrath of Elihu, the son of Barachel the Buzite, of the family of Ram, was aroused against Job; his wrath was aroused because he justified himself rather than God. Also against his three friends his wrath was aroused, because they had found no answer, and yet had condemned Job. Now because they were years older than he, Elihu had waited to speak to Job. When Elihu saw that there was no answer in the mouth of these three men, his wrath was aroused. So Elihu, the son of Barachel the Buzite, answered and said: 'I am young in years, and you are very old; therefore I was afraid, and dared not declare my opinion to you. I said, "Age should speak, and multitude of years should teach wisdom." But there is a spirit in man, and the breath of the Almighty gives him understanding. Great men are not always wise, nor do the aged always understand justice." Therefore I say, listen to me, I also will declare my opinion. Indeed I waited for your words, I listened to your reasonings, while you searched out what to say. I paid close attention to you; and surely not one of you convinced Job, or answered his words—lest you say, "We have found wisdom"; God will vanquish him, not man. Now he has not directed his words against me; so I will not answer him with your words. They are dismayed and answer no more; words escape them. And I have waited, because they did not speak, because they stood still and answered no more. I also will answer my part, I too will declare my opinion. For I am full of words; the spirit within me compels me. Indeed my belly is like wine that has no vent; it is ready to burst like new wineskins. I will speak, that I may find relief; I must open my lips and answer. Let me not, I pray, show partiality to anyone; nor let me flatter any man. For I do not know how to flatter, else my Maker would soon take me away.'"*

Elihu came to Job and said that he had been listening to those conversations all those days and could hardly contain himself anymore. It was rising up within him. He *had* to speak out what he was feeling. He was burning inside with righteous fire from God. Elihu began to share with them what he believed was happening in Job's life.

God is using this young prophet to try to reach Job and bring him to the end of himself. We must all come to the end of ourselves before we can receive the endlessness of the Almighty. Over the years, God has sent me to His servants to deliver a word from Him. Some have received the word and turned back to God's will, but others were too prideful and continued on the wrong path, following their own plans and desires.

I remember one of those times in particular. God had given me a vision of a pastor from our city as I was praying. In the vision I saw the pastor's wife speaking to the congregation. Then I saw the pastor's wife carrying two suitcases out the front doors and down the steps. Next I saw something that was very troubling—a burial casket followed the pastor's wife down the steps, but I never saw the pastor.

After the vision was over, the Lord told me to go and share this vision with the pastor. I did as the Lord instructed me and went to this man and shared exactly what I saw. When I was finished sharing the vision of the Lord, I could see that he was very shaken. He went away and sought all the men of God he knew, asking them for an interpretation, but he never prayed to God himself nor sought God for wisdom. Because of this lack of prayer, God did not reveal the interpretation to this pastor.

The Lord had given me the interpretation of the vision, but He did not tell me what the pastor was doing that would bring this about. The Lord also instructed me not to share the interpretation with the man. Here is the interpretation of the vision that the Lord had given me: The pastor's wife would go before the church to give her husband's resignation. The two suitcases represented his belongings from the church being removed by his wife. The casket was symbolic of spiritual death and not physical death—he would never preach again.

Several months went by and I did not see this man again, but one day I received a phone call from a friend. His first words to me were, "Did you hear what happened to Pastor So-and-So?" and then he proceeded to tell me. This man was caught with a woman from the church other than his wife. The following Sunday his wife went to church to give his resignation; she packed up all his belongings and left with them. The man stopped going to any church. He was never restored and he never preached again, which was represented by the casket, spiritual death.

All of this could have been avoided had he sought God's wisdom on the vision I shared with him, and not run to men for their opinion. It is always tragic when people, especially Christians, sin and refuse to humble themselves. They refuse to come to the end of themselves and repent even when they know they are in sin.

Wisdom Comes from Knowing God

Elihu was obedient to God and delivered God's word to Job, hoping Job would seek God for wisdom in his situation. Things are going to change for Job very soon!

But first, let's read some of the words Elihu spoke to Job, Eliphaz, Bildad, and Zophar, reminding them of the wrong words that had been spoken against God. He reminds them that the words they spoke were very important. (I will be sharing more about our words in the next chapter.)

> *Job 33:8-12,* "*Surely you have spoken in my hearing, and I have heard the sound of your words, saying, 'I am pure, without transgression; I am innocent, and there is no iniquity in me. Yet He finds occasions against me, He counts me as His enemy; He puts my feet in the stocks, He watches all my paths.' Look, in this you are not righteous. I will answer you, for God is greater than man.*"

This young man had an enormous amount of wisdom. Many today do not have that kind of wisdom. Elihu was reiterating what Job had been saying about himself: "There is no iniquity in me. I am pure, without transgression, yet He finds occasions against me. He counts me as His enemy; He puts my feet in the stocks; He watches all my paths." Job found no fault with himself, but he found a way to blame God for his misery.

> *Job 34:10-18,* "*'Therefore listen to me, you men of understanding: Far be it from God to do wickedness, and from the Almighty to commit iniquity. For He repays man according to his work, and makes man to find a reward according to his way. Surely God will never do wickedly, nor will the Almighty pervert justice. Who gave Him charge over the*

earth? Or who appointed Him over the whole world? If He should set His heart on it, if He should gather to Himself His Spirit and His breath, all flesh would perish together, and man would return to dust. If you have understanding, hear this; listen to the sound of my words: Should one who hates justice govern? Will you condemn Him who is most just? Is it fitting to say to a king, "You are worthless," and to nobles, "you are wicked"?"

Elihu informed Job and his friends that it would be far from God to do wickedness and that God does not send evil, disaster, sickness, or anything bad. He also asked them pointed questions about God, like: Who gave Him charge over the earth? Or, who appointed Him over the whole world? If He should set His heart on it, if He should gather to Himself His Spirit and His breath, all flesh would perish together, and man would return to dust.

Elihu said that it was because of the grace and mercy and love of God that the earth was held together. It was the constant outpouring of God's very presence on the earth that kept the earth spinning on its axis and kept the sun, moon, and stars where they were supposed to be. It was the constant concern that God had for the world and for mankind that kept it going. If there was wickedness in Him, it would show up and everything would fall apart. If there was evil and iniquity in Him, the seasons would not come around as they do and the animals would not bear their young like they do. Things would be all out of order. God is so full of love and concern that everything stays in order. There is no wickedness or iniquity in God.

What a wonderful word this is! Every Christian must learn this about God. He is not our problem. He is not troubling us with trials and foiling our endeavors. He is not causing sickness, for He is the Healer and He cannot be both the destroyer and healer. Look at what the apostle Paul wrote in Acts 10:

Acts 10:38, "How God anointed Jesus of Nazareth with the Holy Spirit and with power, who went about doing good and healing all who were oppressed by the devil, for God was with Him."

It says very clearly that God is our Deliverer and Healer. The devil is the oppressor and destroyer. *God and the devil are not working together to get people saved!* God is almighty, and He needs absolutely no help from the filthy, unholy, hell-bound devil!

What Elihu was pointing out here was that if God were worthless and did wicked things, how could He be in charge of the world? God would have to hate justice in order to do all this to Job. Elihu knew that if indeed God did all of that, He would not be able to be God. This man had accurate insight into God. Many Christians need to gain this same insight: God does good—the devil does evil.

> *Job 34:34-37*, "Men of understanding say to me, wise men who listen to me: 'Job speaks without knowledge, his word are without wisdom.' Oh, that Job were tried to the utmost, because his answers are like those of wicked men! For he adds rebellion to his sin; he claps his hands among us, and multiplies his words against God.'"

Elihu had Job's number. He laid it on the line for Job—point blank!

Watch What You Say!

Your words could be killing you. Look at what the writer of Proverbs says about our tongue, lips, and words:

> *Proverbs 18:21*, "Death and life are in the power of the tongue, and those who love it will eat its fruit."

> *Proverbs 10:19-21*, "In the multitude of words sin is not lacking, but he who restrains his lips is wise. The tongue of the righteous is choice silver; the heart of the wicked is worth little. The lips of the righteous feed many, but fools die for lack of wisdom."

> *Job 35:16*, "Therefore Job opens his mouth in vain; he multiplies words without knowledge."

We need to be *very* careful about what we say about God. Young Elihu was a man of God and He rebuked Job for his evil speech. I do not think most people have read this far into the book of Job or paid attention to what Elihu had said about Job.

> ***Psalm 37:30-31****, "The mouth of the righteous speaks wisdom, and his tongue talks of justice. The law of his God is in his heart; none of his steps shall slide."*
>
> ***Psalm 49:3****, "My mouth shall speak wisdom, and the meditation of my heart shall give understanding."*
>
> ***Job 36:2-6****, "Bear with me a little, and I will show you that there are yet words to speak on God's behalf. I will fetch my knowledge from afar; I will ascribe righteousness to my Maker. For truly my words are not false; One who is perfect in knowledge is with you. Behold, God is mighty, but despises no one; He is mighty in strength of understanding. He does not preserve the life of the wicked. But gives justice to the oppressed."*
>
> ***Job 37:21-24****, "Even now men cannot look at the light when it is bright in the skies, when the wind has passed and cleared them. He comes from the north as golden splendor; with God is awesome majesty. As for the Almighty, we cannot find Him; He is excellent in power, in judgment and abundant justice; He does not oppress. Therefore men fear Him; He shows no partiality to any who are wise of heart."*

Nowhere in Elihu's discourse did he mention God sending the devil to mess with Job. Does it say anything about God and the devil being in cahoots with each other to prove anything about Job? Does it say anything about God tempting Job in any way? There was nothing Elihu said by the power of the Holy Spirit that even alluded to God in this way.

Christians need to weigh out the entire book of Job before they make a doctrine out of it and teach it to others. Most folks read the first two chapters and then preach on it. NO! Job was *not* a righteous man—he was a *religious* man who *thought* he was righteous, like so many today.

Job got the wind knocked out of his sails when the Holy Ghost spoke to him through Elihu. He finally realized that he had a gross misunderstanding of God. We have to be sure that we do not share his misunderstandings nor agree with his *initial* opinion of God.

CHAPTER EIGHT

We Live by Our Words

"We live by the words of our mouth." If I had heard that statement before I was saved, it would have meant nothing to me. I must admit that when I was a young believer, it still meant nothing to me; but it is true that *we live by the words of our mouth.*

It was only after I heard the real gospel preached and I listened and studied that I received this message. Of course, the Holy Spirit was my real teacher, showing me how to rightly divide the Word of Truth. I believe that is why the Holy Spirit spoke to me to study and write about Job. I was searching the Word of God for truth, and the Lord said that He would teach me something that He has not revealed to very many people.

In **Job 6:24**, Job says, *"Teach me, and I will hold my tongue; cause me to understand wherein I have erred."* Job knew there was something wrong with his words, but he did not know how to correct them. We want to be very careful of what we speak. I do not think Job started speaking wrong and speaking against God *after* all these disasters; I believe he always spoke wrong about daily life and situations.

See what Jesus said about words and their impact:

> *Matthew 12:33-37, "Either make the tree good and its fruit good, or else make the tree bad and its fruit bad. Brood of vipers! How can you, being evil, speak good things? For out of the abundance of the heart the mouth speaks. A good man out of the good treasure of his heart brings*

forth good things, and an evil man out of the evil treasure brings forth evil things. But I say to you that for every idle word men may speak, they will give account of it in the day of judgment. For by your words you will be justified, and by your words you will be condemned."

In Matthew 12:33, Jesus was not talking about trees and fruit; He was saying that you can judge a person's life by the words he speaks and what his words produce. This is what I want to show you in this chapter. It is our words that decide the outcome of our life. Words have power.

In Matthew 12:34-35, Jesus said that you can tell what is in a person's heart by what comes out of their mouth. Have you ever been around someone who hit their thumb with a hammer, or something else painful or unpleasant happened, and immediately they cursed a blue streak? That tells you what is in their heart. A Christian, on the other hand, will say, "Praise God, I'm healed by Christ's stripes!" or just, "Ouch!" because that is what is in their heart.

Matthew 12:36 says that we will be judged for our idle words. The word "idle" has the meaning of worthless. Jesus never spoke an idle word. All His words had truth, life, and meaning. All the words we have ever spoken are recorded in heaven. If you have spoken some worthless or untrue words, you can repent and ask God for forgiveness, and then start speaking living, fruitful words.

In Matthew 12:37, we see that we will be justified or condemned by our words. God, the Great Judge, will judge us on what we say. Our words must be faith-filled words based on God's Word, and not based on doubt and unbelief. Our words, when they align with God's Word, have the power and blessing of God to produce a successful, peace-filled, happy life.

Proverbs 18:21, "Death and life are in the power of the tongue, and those who love it will eat its fruit."

We can speak doubt, worry, unbelief, gossip, lies, and negative words which will not only bring evil to us, but can eventually kill us. This is how the world speaks, but as Christians we can speak life and should *only* speak life.

Proverbs 13:2-3, "A man shall eat well by the fruit of his mouth, but the soul of the unfaithful feeds on violence. He who guards his mouth preserves his life, but he who opens wide his lips shall have destruction."

This tells us that our words are important and will make a difference. Our words of faith will cause us to be successful. I have hundreds of examples of this in my life. There are two very powerful things God has taught me that bring good into my life: (1) My level of giving in tithes and offerings, and (2) The words I speak, which are the same words I find that God has spoken.

The Christian life consists of many truths, including living a holy life, being a forgiver, walking in love toward others, and always praising and worshiping God. We all need to be what God has intended us to be.

The power of giving God the tithe and offerings, and speaking God-ordained words has made a huge impact on my life and ministry. These aspects are often overlooked in people's lives, which could explain why things are not going the way they would like.

I remember when we bought 12 acres of prime land on which to build our church's worship center. We had no money and very few people. But I had something far more valuable than money—I had God's Word. Money is only a commodity of this natural world, but God's Word is more precious than silver and gold. The Word of God is based on the economy of heaven, where there is no lack. So I have found that if I believe what the Bible says and speak it out by faith, I will have what I say.

Now some Christians may get upset with that statement, but please do not stop reading now. Wouldn't you love to have the keys of the kingdom of God to unlock the mysteries of God's Word? Now is your chance.

We bought 12 acres of the most prime real estate in our city on I-35 on Spirit Mountain; the most beautiful part of our region. I would walk on the land when there were still only trees and brush, and I would speak to it. I would tell the building where it would stand. I would speak to the walls and roof and tell them to come forth in Jesus' name. I would tell the platform where it would be. I prophesied people coming and many people from foreign countries coming as well. I called for thousands of salvations, healings, and deliverances. I knew it was God's plan to put us on the highest point in our whole region, where thousands of motorists pass by each day. These people had the awesome opportunity to watch a miracle of God take place. Without any bank financing in place, only $40,000 in donations, and a loan from a church member, we built a first-class 10,000 square foot worship center—and then the people came.

There is a McDonald's restaurant next to our property. They were very happy for us and donated 2.5 acres of adjoining land, which brings us to 14.5 acres. This is one of the most beautiful settings I know of, with huge trees and rocks, and a 1,000 foot winding driveway through the woods leading to our worship center.

I knew that faith-filled words had to be spoken before the land could be obtained or the building completed. God has honored those words.

Speak the Word.
So far in this chapter we have learned that death and life are in the tongue, which means that the negative and critical words we speak can kill. When we speak words in faith that agree with the Bible, it brings life to us. I see so many who are sad, discouraged, hopeless, and see no way out of the situations they are in. Even many Christians are that way; but if they would change their thinking and realize that God is their help and not their trouble, they would see change for the better. If they just understood that God did not send Jesus to the earth to make them sad, discouraged, and hopeless, but that He came that they might have life, then God would be able to actually show Himself strong on their behalf.

> ***John 10:10 (Amp)****, "The thief comes only in order to steal and kill and destroy. I came that they may have and enjoy life, and have it in abundance (to the full, till it overflows)."*

I want to share a very powerful verse that Jesus spoke. You should read the whole eleventh chapter of Mark where the account of Jesus cursing the fig tree is found. As they passed that way the very next day, the disciples were amazed when they saw that the fig tree that Jesus had cursed was completely dried up from the roots.

*Mark 11:21-22, "And Peter, remembering, said to Him, 'Rabbi, look! The fig tree which You cursed has withered away.' So Jesus answered and said to them, **'Have faith in God'**" (emphasis added).*

That seems like a simple enough command, but many never get it. They go through life having faith in money, people, employers, politicians, their education, their social status, and, of course, themselves, all of which can and will fail them. But the One who will never fail them they never totally trust. God said:

Deuteronomy 31:6, "Be strong and of good courage, do not fear nor be afraid of them; for the Lord your God, He is the One who goes with you. He will not leave you nor forsake you."

He is the one I will put my faith in!

In Mark 11, Jesus goes on to tell us how we, too, may have power in our mouths which will bring such results:

Mark 11:23-24, "For assuredly, I say to you, whoever says to this mountain, 'Be removed and be cast into the sea,' and does not doubt in his heart, but believes that those things he says will be done, he will have whatever he says. Therefore I say to you, whatever things you ask when you pray, believe that you receive them, and you will have them."

Jesus said *"assuredly, I say."* First of all, the word "assuredly" is the same as the word for promise. So Jesus is telling us that He promises that the words He says to us are true. Secondly, He uses the word **"say"** five times. To "say" means to speak words. You cannot *say* anything without words.

The word "whoever" includes you, me, and anyone else who believes and does not doubt in his heart. Jesus said, *"whoever **says** to this mountain* [He was probably motioning to a nearby mountain] *'Be removed and cast into the sea,' and does not doubt in his heart, but believes that those things he **says** will be done, he will have whatever he **says**."*

Now a mountain can also refer to a hindrance in our lives such as sickness, lack, or any other kind of problem. Jesus says that we first need to have faith in God and then speak to the problem (mountain) be it sickness, lack of goods, lack of money, etc., and it *must* obey our words and not remain in our life. It *must* go. And if it is something we need, it *must* come to us.

Remember the Roman centurion whose servant was dying? He came to Jesus and said that he was not worthy of the Lord coming to his house, but went on to say that if Jesus would just say the word, he knew his servant would be healed.

> *Matthew 8:5-13, "Now when Jesus had entered Capernaum, a centurion came to him, pleading with Him, saying, 'Lord, my servant is lying at home paralyzed, dreadfully tormented.' And Jesus said to him, 'I will come and heal him.' The centurion answered and said, 'Lord, I am not worthy that You should come under my roof. But only speak a word, and my servant will be healed. For I also am a man under authority, having soldiers under me. And I say to this one, "Go," and he goes; and to another, "Come," and he comes; and to my servant, "do this," and he does it.' When Jesus heard it, He marveled, and said to those who followed, 'Assuredly, I say to you, I have not found such great faith, not even in Israel! And I say to you that many will come from east and west, and sit down with Abraham, Isaac, and Jacob in the kingdom of heaven. But the sons of the kingdom will be cast out into outer darkness. There will be weeping and gnashing of teeth.' Then Jesus said to the centurion, 'Go your way; and as you have believed, so let it be done for you.' And his servant was healed that same hour."*

Jesus was very touched by this Roman's faith. He said that He had not seen faith like that in all of Israel. That is a very sad statement. Jesus said that this Roman military officer had more faith than the religious leaders and most of the people.

In regard to having faith, Jesus asks a question in Luke 18:8 that is a huge issue for the church today:

> *Luke 18:8b, "Nevertheless, when the Son of man comes, will He really find faith on the earth?"*

I see less and less faith in churches today. We must stop trusting the world system, which is a failed system, and we need to put our faith back in God and His Word.

The key to great faith
In Mark 11:23, we see the main key to great faith:

> *Mark 11:23b*, "… and does not doubt in his heart …"

Faith comes out of the heart, so if doubt resides in our heart about a particular thing, faith cannot reside there too. We need to continually be filled with the Word of God, believe it, and then we will have faith.

> **Romans 10:17**, *"So then faith comes by hearing, and hearing by the word of God."*

Jesus did this wonderful teaching about speaking by faith because He spoke to the fig tree that had no fruit and said:

> **Mark 11:14**, *"'Let no one eat fruit from you ever again.' And His disciples heard it."*

Now, Jesus could have just as easily blessed the fig tree and told fruit to come forth from it, but He was using the fig tree as a type of symbolism. The fig tree represented Israel. The leaves were a sign that there should already have been fruit on the tree. Israel was very religious; the Pharisees and Sadducees were like the fig tree, because they had a lot of "leaves" but no fruit in their lives. They had no true faith in their religion. They were cursed, dried up, and never produced any fruit. Jesus did not make this dead religion become fruitful; He let it dry up. And so it is with dead religions today—where there is no faith there is no fruit.

Build your faith
Even back in Job's day some people understood the power of the spoken word. Eliphaz said:

> **Job 22:28**, *"You will also declare a thing, and it will be established for you; so light will shine on your ways."*

He knew that if you declared something by faith, it would come to pass. Start living this way and watch your life change.

Do you remember what Job said in Job chapter 6?

Job 6:24, "Teach me, and I will hold my tongue; cause me to understand wherein I have erred."

He should have prayed that *before* all the tragedy struck. Many people have a weak, almost nonexistent, faith-walk. So, when the devil strikes these people, they are not only fighting the battle, but they are also trying to build their faith at the same time.

The time to build your faith is *before* the battle. A boxer does not learn how to box in the ring fighting against his opponent. He learned how to fight at the gym with a trainer who helped him build his strength and technique. Your trainer is the Holy Ghost; let Him lead you in the life of faith so you can be pleasing to God.

Hebrews 11:6, "But without faith it is impossible to please Him, for he who comes to God must believe that He is, and that He is a rewarder of those who diligently seek Him."

CHAPTER NINE

God Shows Up

Finally God Shows Up!

Job 38:1-7, "Then the Lord answered Job out of the whirlwind, and said: 'Who is this who darkens counsel by words without knowledge? Now prepare yourself like a man; I will question you, and you shall answer Me. Where were you when I laid the foundations of the earth? Tell Me, if you have understanding. Who determined its measurements? Surely you know! Or who stretched the line upon it? To what were its foundations fastened? Or who laid its cornerstone, when the morning stars sang together, and all the sons of God shouted for joy?'"

In Job 38:2, God was talking to Job. He was telling Job that he had no knowledge of God. Job had been expressing his opinions of God and aligning himself with traditional beliefs about God.

It was a similar scenario when Jesus was on the earth. He was constantly dealing with the Pharisees. They were the only ministers around at the time and they had created a false hierarchy in the synagogue. They had beliefs and teachings about God that were wrong. Jesus lays it all out on the table about the Pharisees in a number of places; some of the more well-defined accounts are in Luke 11 and in Mathew 12 and 23, but Matthew 23:27 sums up the scribes and Pharisees like this:

Matthew 23:27, "Woe to you, scribes and Pharisees, hypocrites! For you are like white-washed tombs which indeed appear beautiful outwardly, but inside are full of dead men's bones and all uncleanness."

Job is put on the spot.
In Job 38, we see that God was not happy that Job had said all those wrong things about Him. He told Job to pull himself together, clean himself up, prepare himself like a man, and answer Him. God challenged Job. Being that Job thought he knew God so well, God asked Him very pointed questions and told him to give Him the answers.

> *Job 38:4-5a,* "*Where were you when I laid the foundations of the earth? Tell Me, if you have understanding. Who determined its measurements? Surely you know!*"

God really put him on the spot. In essence, He was asking Job, "Who are *you* to falsely blame *Me* for what has gone wrong in your life?" Good question!

> *Job 39:1-4,* "*Do you know the time when the wild mountain goats bear young? Or can you mark when the deer gives birth? Can you number the months that they fulfill? Or do you know the time when they bear young? They bow down, they bring forth their young, they deliver their offspring. Their young ones are healthy, they grow strong with grain; they depart and do not return to them.*'"

Wow! Just take a moment and try to comprehend what God has created. He knows the smallest details of nature and cares immensely about all His creation. Doing this will keep your relationship with God in proper perspective.

God is making it clear to Job that He has everything under control; He has set everything in order. God makes it clear to Job that He is a *good* God. He cares about the smallest detail of all His creation. If He cares so much for the creatures of the earth, how much more does He care for us who have been made in His own image!

Jesus makes that same point very clear in Matthew 6 where we see Him saying that His heavenly Father cares about the birds of the air and the flowers of the field:

> *Matthew 6:25-30,* "*Therefore I say to you, do not worry about your life, what you will eat or what you will drink; nor about your body,*

what you will put on. Is not life more than food and the body more than clothing? Look at the birds of the air, for they neither sow nor reap nor gather into barns; yet your heavenly Father feeds them. Are you not of more value than they? Which of you by worrying can add one cubit to his stature? So why do you worry about clothing? Consider the lilies of the field, how they grow; they neither toil nor spin; and yet I say to you that even Solomon in all his glory was not arrayed like one of these. Now if God so clothes the grass of the field, which today is, and tomorrow is thrown into the oven, will He not much more clothe you, O you of little faith?"

God is for us.

We should never forget how much God cares for us and loves us. How could anyone ever think that God would send trouble, sickness, and poverty on us? He does not do things to us just to see what we will do about it. That would go against His very nature!

> ***1 Corinthians 10:13**, "No temptation has overtaken you except such as is common to man; but God is faithful, who will not allow you to be tempted beyond what you are able, but with the temptation will also make the way of escape, that you may be able to bear it."*

This passage tells us that God will not let us be tempted beyond what we can handle. It does *not* say He sends the temptation. He says that He will be there to help us. We *will* face tests and trials as Christians, but these are testings of our faith.

Man is not in charge of the earth.

As we see in the following passage, *God* is in charge of all things in regard to nature and the earth; contrary to popular belief, man is not:

> ***Job 39:19, 26-27**, "Have you given the horse strength? Have you clothed his neck with thunder? Does the hawk fly by your wisdom, and spread its wings toward the south? Does the eagle mount up at your command, and make its nest on high?"*

Lately, we have been hearing much talk about global warming and the cause of it. These people think they can control our earth's weather and climate. They deny that the weather has only warmed up 7/8 of a degree in the past 100 years. That may very well be God's plan. They also refuse to look at the fact that man only causes about 3% of all CO_2 gases; the other 97% is caused by nature.

The Lord spoke to me recently and said that these men are fools and do not understand that He is in control of the weather. He said that *He* is God, not Al Gore; and that is the same message God was getting across to Job: "I am God and you are not, Job!"

Contending with God Is Dangerous

> *Job 40:1-2, "Moreover the Lord answered Job, and said: 'Shall the one who contends with the Almighty correct Him? He who rebukes God, let him answer it."*

God said that Job actually rebuked Him and contended with Him! Contending with someone means that you are in a fight with them. God told Job in no uncertain terms that he was wrong. Do not let anyone tell you differently. God was very upset with Job!

There are three kinds of occasions in the Bible when God shows up: (1) When He wants to give you a message and send you on your way to deliver it, (2) to give you a blessing, and (3) when He wants to correct you. When He showed up in Job's life, it was to set Job straight about Him; it was to correct him big time!

> *Job 40:3-14, "Then Job answered the Lord and said: 'Behold, I am vile; what shall I answer You? I lay my hand over my mouth. Once I have spoken, but I will not answer; yes, twice, but I will proceed no further.' Then the Lord answered Job out of the whirlwind, and said: 'Now prepare yourself like a man; I will question you, and you shall answer Me: Would you indeed annul My judgment? Would you condemn Me that you may be justified? Have you an arm like God? Or can you thunder with a voice like His? Then adorn yourself with majesty and splendor, and array yourself with glory and beauty. Disperse the rage of your wrath; look on everyone who is proud, and bring him low; tread down the wicked in their place. Hide them in the dust together, bind their faces in hidden darkness. Then I will also confess to you that your own right hand can save you.'"*

God Shows Up

Being vile is just about the worst condition a person can be in. Job realized just who he was when he actually met the living God. He realized that he was lower than dirt, and that he amounted to nothing in his own ability. God told Job that if he could make himself glorious and beautiful then He, God, would confess to Job that he, Job, was indeed something and capable of saving himself. Do you sense God's tone of voice being a little challenging to Job? I am trying to put it nicely.

God continues to talk about His creation and all the wonderful things that He does. Then in chapter 42 we see Job's reaction to his encounter with God.

CHAPTER TEN

Repentance Is a Fresh Start

Job Has an Encounter with God

As a reminder, in Job 1:21 we recall Job saying, "*'Naked I came from my mother's womb, and naked shall I return there. The Lord gave, and the Lord has taken away; blessed be the name of the Lord.'*" But now in Job 42, we see a different confession. Here we find one of the main lessons to be learned from the book of Job:

> *Job 42:1-3, "Then Job answered the Lord and said: 'I know that You can do everything, and that no purpose of Yours can be withheld from You. You asked, "Who is this who hides counsel without knowledge?" Therefore I have uttered what I did not understand, things too wonderful for me, which I did not know.'"*

Job admitted that he had falsely accused God. Seventy-four times he accused God falsely. He did not understand God. Job was sorry for his foolish words.

> *Job 42:5, "I have heard of You by the hearing of the ear, but now my eye sees You."*

In essence, Job was saying, "I have heard of you by my ear (this was from tradition), but I have never experienced a personal relationship with You. But now I see You with my eyes. My spiritual eyes are open. Now I see God."

Repentance Is a Fresh Start

Job Repents

After all these things happened, and Elihu gave him counsel, God spoke to him and corrected him. Job said, "Now I know You. Now I know You would not put destruction and evil upon a man. Therefore I abhor myself." Job starts to repent here, which opens the door for him to be able to learn.

> *Job 42:6*, "*Therefore I abhor myself, and repent in dust and ashes.*"

He got rid of his pride, rebellion, and religion, and became a true believer in the living God. It was like he was saying, "I am ashamed of myself for my attitude, for my lousy thinking, for all the false accusations that I made about You, God. For now I know You are a God that is mighty, powerful, full of love, and who would not do these things to a man; please forgive me."

When we finally surrender to God and humble ourselves, we too can receive wisdom that only comes from Him.

> *Proverbs 9:10*, "*The fear of the Lord is the beginning of wisdom, and the knowledge of the Holy One is understanding.*"

> *Job 42:1-6*, "*Then Job answered the Lord and said: 'I know that You can do everything, and that no purpose of Yours can be withheld from You. You asked, "Who is this who hides counsel without knowledge?" Therefore I have uttered what I did not understand, things too wonderful for me, which I did not know. Listen, please, and let me speak; You said, "I will question you, and you shall answer Me." I have heard of You by the hearing of the ear, but now my eye sees you. Therefore I abhor myself, and repent in dust and ashes.'*"

Look at that! Job admitted that he was a religious man and that he had only *heard* things about God and believed them, but he never *knew* Him until now. That is how it is with so many people. They know *about* God, but they have never had a personal encounter with Him—they do not *know* Him. It is like someone saying today that they know George Washington, Abraham Lincoln, or some other famous person in history that they have read about. Yes, they may have read and heard a lot *about* these men. They may know their birthday, where they lived, and they may even be able to tell of all the good works they did, but they cannot say they actually *know* them.

We need to have an actual encounter with God. We need to have an ongoing, personal relationship with Him that grows deeper and continually gets better on a daily basis. The day that you were born again was wonderful and moving, but ten years later you should be different. You should not be in the same place spiritually as you were when you were first born again; your overall maturity level should have improved as well.

If you have not grown closer to God and matured, it is because you have not been seeking God and chasing after Him. You have not been taking the needed time to get close to Him, listen to Him, and know Him.

Become intimate with God.
Our relationship with God is very much like a marriage. A marriage is not a marriage until the man and woman have been intimate with each other. The marriage will not become strong and healthy unless there is ongoing, regular intimacy. Many marriages have failed for different reasons, but one reason we often hear is that the couple grew apart. Part of that is that their intimacy with each other came to an end, which is usually a result of one of them pulling away.

If we fail to draw closer to God and be intimate with Him, then we too will grow apart from Him. God never pulls away from us, we pull away from Him. God never fails us, we fail ourselves and God.

If this has happened to you, then this would be the time to come back and restore your relationship with Jesus. Start by repenting for your waywardness, asking for forgiveness, and that you may be restored again unto right standing with almighty God.

Job's fourth friend

> *Job 42:7, "And so it was, after the Lord had spoken these words to Job, that the Lord said to Eliphaz the Temanite, 'My wrath is aroused against you and your two friends, for you have not spoken of Me what is right, as My servant Job has.'"*

Remember there were four friends with Job. We see here that God was angry with the first three friends. However, God's wrath was not kindled against Elihu, the young man who actually *did* have a relationship with God and actually did *know* Him. Why wasn't God angry with Elihu? Because Elihu was right! Elihu was burning up, ready to burst with the Holy Ghost. Elihu spoke in God's defense and confronted Job with the fact that he was wrong about God. That is what opened the door for Job's understanding of God.

Elihu was a wise young man. Job was bound up in religion and tradition; he was void of a relationship with God, but not so with Elihu. He was a God-seeker and a God-pleaser.

You have to become that kind of an individual on purpose. You need to purpose in your heart to know God no matter what it takes. You need to not be satisfied until you reach the secret place of the Most High and fellowship with God there. Religion is no substitute for relationship.

You have to be born again.
You may not understand what I'm saying here if you have been basing your relationship with God on some form of religion. It may be because you are not truly born again in the way that Jesus said one had to be in order to spend eternity in heaven with Him.

> *John 3:1-3, "There was a man of the Pharisees named Nicodemus, a ruler of the Jews. This man came to Jesus by night and said to Him, 'Rabbi, we know that Your are a teacher come from God; for no one can do these signs that You do unless God is with him.' Jesus answered and said to him, 'Most assuredly, I say to you, unless one is born again, he cannot see the kingdom of God.'"*

If this is the case, and you are not born again, it would be very good to take a few moments to pray right now with all sincerity and openness to Jesus. Ask Him to forgive you, a sinner, and to come into your heart and be your Lord and Savior. When you have done that, you can begin your new born again life!

> *2 Peter 3:9, 17-18,* "*The Lord is not slack concerning His promise, as some count slackness, but is longsuffering toward us, not willing that any should perish but that all should come to repentance.*"
>
> "*You therefore, beloved, since you know this beforehand, beware lest you also fall from your own steadfastness, being led away with the error of the wicked; but grow in the grace and knowledge of our Lord and Savior Jesus Christ. To Him be the glory both now and forever. Amen.*"

We see in this passage that God desires every human being to be saved and come to the knowledge of Jesus Christ. He would love for everyone to have an even closer relationship with Him than Elihu had.

The other three friends

> *Job 42:8-13,* "*'Now therefore, take for yourselves seven bulls and seven rams, go to My servant Job, and offer up for yourselves a burnt offering; and my servant Job shall pray for you.* **For I will accept him, lest I deal with you according to your folly; because you have not spoken of Me what is right, as My servant Job has.**' *So Eliphaz the Temanite and Bildad the Shuhite and Zophar the Naamathite went and did as the Lord commanded them; for the Lord had accepted Job.* **And the Lord restored Job's losses when he prayed for his friends. Indeed the Lord gave Job twice as much as he had before.** *Then all his brothers, all his sisters, and all those who had been his acquaintances before, came to him and ate food with him in his house; and they consoled him and comforted him for all the adversity that the Lord had brought upon him. Each one gave him a piece of silver and each a ring of gold. Now the Lord blessed the latter days of Job more than his beginning; for he had fourteen thousand sheep, six thousand camels, one thousand yoke of oxen, and one thousand female donkeys. He also had seven sons and three daughters*" (emphasis added).

In Job 42:9, God said He would accept Job. Isn't God a loving, merciful God? Job had accused God wrongly for months. Job blamed God for all his troubles, and when God finally challenged Job's wrong accusations, Job repented.

> *Job 42:6,* "*Therefore I abhor myself, and repent in dust and ashes.*"

If we are not careful and spiritual, we can go through life with wrong assumptions and opinions of God. This is why we must seek God and be intimate with Him, so we can receive His truth through the Holy Spirit and His Word, for His Word is life.

There are many different ideas about God in the church world. Some of these are so far from the truth that they are actually lies about God. My friends, this should not be so. God is not speaking any lies; He always speaks in agreement with His Word as it is found in the Bible. God also has not formed a single denomination. He is not interested in denominationalism. He is interested in truth and His Word is truth. We must put God's Word above every idea and opinion of man that is contrary to it.

We must humble ourselves and say, "Oh, God, have mercy on me. I am but dust, and what can I know unless You teach me and guide me into all Your truth?" When we become humble and teachable, then, and only then, will God reveal His truth to us.

It is interesting that God will not *force* His truth on us. He will send ministers of righteousness and believers who are full of the truth to help us. However, God won't force us to change our thinking if we refuse to listen to them, and He will not be able to completely bless us and meet our every need and desire if we don't heed the voice of His Word spoken through His trustworthy servants.

Results of Job's repentance
When Job humbled himself, repented, and got right with God, God restored a double portion back to him! When we do the same thing, God will restore more unto us. It is God's desire to bless us.

In Job 42:7, we see that God had spoken to Job's three friends, Eliphaz, Bildad, and Zophar. He told them that they had not spoken right of Him as Job did. Basically, Job just repented for his bad doctrine (belief system about God), and God forgave him.

Job's three friends were obedient and did as God said. By doing so, they were spared any further correction from God.

In Job 42:10, the Lord restored Job's losses when he prayed for his three friends who had become like enemies to him. This showed that Job had forgiven them. They had said some mean, judgmental things about Job, but he genuinely forgave them.

Because Job actually knew God, he walked in the truth that Jesus spoke hundreds of years later in Matthew 5 where it says that we are to pray for our enemies.

> *Matthew 5:44,* "But I say to you, love your enemies, bless those who curse you, do good to those who hate you, and pray for those who spitefully use you and persecute you."

If Job had not brought himself to pray for these men, then God could not have blessed and restored Job's life. Job was a good man who thought he knew God. He had just been wrongly taught.

Job became a very good example to the church: (1) He was quick to humble himself, (2) he was quick to repent when he realized he was wrong, (3) he was quick to believe God's word, (4) he was quick to obey God, and (5) he was quick to forgive his enemies.

Look what the Lord did for Job because he earnestly did those things. The *Lord* gave him twice as much as he had. The value of his new flocks and herds would be well over one million dollars today. Anyone with a million dollars, debt free, in livestock is in good financial condition. Each year Job's cattle and flocks could have almost doubled, so in five years he would have been extremely rich; plus he had all the silver and gold his brothers, sisters, and acquaintances gave him.

God is not a respecter of persons. If we will believe and conduct ourselves like the new Job of chapter 42, who was (1) humble, (2) quick to repent, (3) quick to believe God's word, (4) quick to obey God, and (5) quick to forgive, then God can bless our lives and restore all that the devil has stolen from us. God can double it, triple it, or increase it one hundred times because He operates by multiplication.

***Psalm 35:27**, "Let them shout for joy and be glad, who favor my righteous cause; and let them say continually, 'Let the Lord be magnified, who has pleasure in the prosperity of His servant.'"*

If God takes pleasure in the prosperity of His servants, how much more pleasure does He have in his sons and daughters? There is no end to what God will do for those who love Him with all their heart, all their mind, all their strength, and who obey Him. The world has yet to see all the blessings God will bestow on His obedient children. God is *not* your trouble!

CHAPTER ELEVEN

The Real Nature of God

Know God through His Word and His Son

I want to share with you eight names of God. These names reveal His nature and character. If you want to know God you have to look in the Word and see who He is. You have to see what His nature is. Here is a list of some of the names of God:

- Jehovah Tsidkenu—God is our righteousness.
- Jehovah M'Kaddesh—Jehovah who sanctifies. He sets us apart for Himself.
- Jehovah Shalom—God is peace.
- Jehovah Shammah—God is there.
- Jehovah Rophe—God heals.
- Jehovah Jireh—God's provision shall be seen.
- Jehovah Nissi—God is my banner.
- Jehovah Rohi—God is my shepherd.

No place in there do we see "God is my destroyer" or "God is my wickedness." No place in that list do we see "God is my lack" or "God is my deficiency." You do not see those traits because those are the devil's traits, not God's.

However, the Bible makes it clear that God *will* punish those who rebel against Him; He *will* destroy those who lie, fight against Him, and cause trouble for His children.

The devil has done a good job of getting people to blame God for their troubles. I had a conversation with a man who had lost his wife to cancer. He said that she was a good Christian. This man had very little knowledge of the Bible, and he said he prayed and asked God to put the cancer his wife had onto him. I could see that the man loved and had compassion on his wife, but no knowledge of God.

First of all, God didn't put the cancer on his wife; cancer is not from God, He does not have any cancer to give anyone. Second, God wanted this lady to be healed. When this man's wife died, he became very angry with God and blamed Him for killing his wife. I shared with the man that God did not kill his wife, but that the devil did. He became a little indignant with me and said, "Why would the devil do that?" Because that is what the devil does! Always remember the devil is a bad spirit, and God is a great God.

> *John 3:16-17*, *"For God so loved the world that He gave His only begotten Son, that whoever believes in Him should not perish but have everlasting life. For God did not send His Son into the world to condemn the world, but that the world through Him might be saved."*
>
> *John 10:10 (Amp)*, *"The thief comes only in order to steal and kill and destroy. I came that they may have and enjoy life, and have it in abundance (to the full, till it overflows)."*

The thief is the devil.

We must exercise faith in God to receive His promises. We must continually study and hear God's Word in order to build our faith in God.

> *Romans 10:17*, *"So then faith comes by hearing, and hearing by the word of God."*

We must also remember that it is God's greatest desire for His children to receive all the blessings and healings He has provided. He wants to take care of His people and His church. He wants to take care of those who believe in Him. God does watch over those who love Him.

If you want to know what the Father is like, look at the Son. Jesus said that no one comes to the Father except through Him. This holds true for not only spending eternity with the Father, but also getting to know Him while still on earth.

> **Hebrews 1:3,** *"Who being the brightness of His glory and the express image of His person, and upholding all things by the word of His power, when He had by Himself purged our sins, sat down at the right hand of the Majesty on high."*

> **Colossians 1:15,** *"He is the image of the invisible God, the firstborn over all creation."*

Jesus Christ is the express image of the Father. When you look at Jesus in the Gospels, you are seeing the image of the heavenly Father in a human body. Jesus said that He did not say or do anything except what He heard and saw His Father do. He was not just a free agent over in Jerusalem. He was not on a hit-and-miss program. He had a plan. He had *God's* plan. He had *God's* mission.

> **John 3:17,** *"For God did not send His Son into the world to condemn the world, but that the world through Him might be saved."*

Jesus came to fulfill our heavenly Father's will and not His own will. Whose will are you trying to fulfill—your own or God's? If you do God's will then He will satisfy and fulfill your desires because His desires become your desires.

Jesus was already ruling with the Father back in Job's day. Do you think Jesus turned Job over to the devil? No, because He loved man as much then as He does today.

> **John 10:30,** *"I and My Father are one."*

> **Luke 9:56,** *"For the Son of Man did not come to destroy men's lives but to save them."*

> **John 3:16,** *"For God so loved the world that He gave His only begotten Son, that whoever believes in Him should not perish but have everlasting life."*

God loved man so much that He was willing to allow His only begotten Son to suffer and become sin for us; He became our only acceptable sacrifice. Jesus did not come to condemn the world, but to save it. This was the Father's plan.

Our Ministry Today

Acts 26:15-18, "'So I said, "Who are You, Lord?" And He said, "I am Jesus, whom you are persecuting. But rise and stand on your feet; for I have appeared to you for this purpose, to make you a minister and a witness both of the things which you have seen and of the things which I will yet reveal to you. I will deliver you from the Jewish people, as well as from the Gentiles, to whom I now send you, to open their eyes, in order to turn them from darkness to light, and from the power of Satan to God, that they may receive forgiveness of sins and an inheritance among those who are sanctified by faith in Me."'

This was the apostle Paul's ministry—to open their spiritual eyes in order to see who God was; to take them from darkness to light and from the power of satan to God. The word "power" in verse 18 has the same meaning as the word "power" used in Job 1:12, which means "in your hand." So we see that Job was already in satan's hand and that he already had power over Job.

The ministry of the apostle Paul, as well as our ministry today, is to deliver people from the hand (power) and authority of satan and bring them into the power of God. People are already under the power of satan from birth. However, that changes when they become born again; they come under the power of the living God. Our ministry is to turn those people from darkness and satan's power, open their eyes, and get them to come into the power of God so that they may receive forgiveness of their sins as well as receive the inheritance of those who are sanctified by faith in Jesus.

God cares deeply about His creation. He loves what He has created. Do you think He would send calamity to an individual to destroy them just because He wants to test their faith? No. Our faith will take us through calamity and troubles, but they are not from God. God is not our trouble, He is our Deliverer.

Walk in Faith in God's Word

In these last days we are going to have to believe unswervingly on God's Word. We need to uphold God, honor Him, tell others that God does not do evil things to us, and that He does not wish for us to have troubles and trials in our lives. He has given us authority and a way to dispel the works of the devil and live a victorious life.

Look at what Jesus said in Luke 10:19 when the 70 disciples returned from their mission trip:

> **Luke 10:19**, *"Behold, I give you the authority to trample on serpents and scorpions, and over all the power of the enemy, and nothing shall by any means hurt you."*

Jesus Himself said that He has given us authority over all the power of the devil. This has been a pivotal Scripture for me for many years. I fully believe what Jesus said and I fully intend to use all the authority that God has given me. Let me tell you that I have had many opportunities to use my God-given authority over the devil. We are to be the devil's boss. He cannot move without our permission. This is why it is so crucial for us to watch our words. We give the devil permission when we speak unbelief, doubt, and negative words. But we keep him bound and powerless when we agree with God's Word and speak faith.

We have an awesome place in God's kingdom that the devil cannot enter. He was in God's kingdom until he rebelled and was thrown out of heaven. Now, through the new birth, we get to serve with Jesus with whom we are joint heirs. The devil can only look in at us and wish he had never sinned and lost his position, which we now possess.

The word "authority" in Luke 10:19, means, "all power." The word "power" comes from the Greek word *exusia*; authority means the right to exercise power, or another way to explain authority is to say, "We can possess the gate of the enemy." I do not know about you, but that excites me!

For years Christians have been crying about the devil troubling them and causing them so much difficulty. This should not be, if we know what the Word says and what our authority is over the devil.

The Real Nature of God

The following is a good way to read Luke 10:19, Behold I give you authority—the right to exercise all power to possess the gate of your enemy—so you will be able to trample on demons and demonic power; and over all the limited power of the enemy. Nothing shall by any means hurt you! When you believe this word from Jesus, your spiritual and natural life will change. You will become victorious and more than a conqueror in Christ Jesus.

> *Romans 8:37-39, "Yet in all these things we are more than conquerors through Him who loved us. For I am persuaded that neither death nor life, nor angels nor principalities nor powers, nor things present nor things to come, nor height nor depth, nor any other created thing, shall be able to separate us from the love of God which is in Christ Jesus our Lord."*

There are people who are still "going through it" years after the trials and troubles had begun. Don't you think they should have come out the other side of "it" by this time? When their doctrine is that God puts things on them to test them, it is no wonder they never "pass the test." Or, if they think that God puts things on them to teach them something—why don't they learn and get over it then? It is because they are in the wrong place with God. God cannot help them very much with such a mind-set; it closes the door for the Holy Spirit to come in and work, and it opens the door for the devil to come in and mess with them. These people are good, well-meaning people who are following a false doctrine.

God's wrath is kindled toward people who speak, preach, and believe like that. God loves them even in their ignorance; He does not strike them dead, but He *does* want them to know and understand the truth. Didn't He love us in our ignorance, while we were still sinners? Doesn't He love us now even when we make mistakes and sin? Yes! God wants us to read and understand His Word from *His* perspective, not our own. Our doctrine cannot be based on our opinion, neither can it be based on someone else's.

God wants to send us blessings. God sent us His only begotten Son, Jesus Christ, to deliver us from death, sickness, and all the strongholds, attacks, and destructions of satan. God hates the devil, and so should we!

We Do Not Listen to the Accuser of the Brethren

Let's go back toward the beginning of Job and review God's relationship with satan.

> *Job 2:1, "Again there was a day when the sons of God came to present themselves before the Lord, and Satan came also among them to present himself before the Lord."*

We need to realize that God does not listen to the "accuser of the brethren." We also need *not* listen to him. When we hear gossip and accusations about one another, we need to cut off the conversation immediately. God turns a deaf ear to all accusations against the brethren, and we need to do the same.

Isaiah 54:17 says that God has even given us the authority to condemn lies and false accusations spoken against us. Isn't God awesome? He always makes a way for us to be delivered and victorious. A weapon is anything sent to harm us, like sickness, disease, poverty, and trouble from people. Wrong words can cause us much damage, but we get to condemn them. We have the authority to do that!

God is out there giving us faith, encouraging us, and showing us how to live a holy life. He is showing us how to live above temptation and the attacks of the devil, how not to be taken in, how to speak His Word over situations, and how to take authority over the devil and all his activities. That is what we are *supposed* to be learning from this book of the Bible, *not* how to make excuses for the bad things happening in our lives and falsely accuse God for them, but to recognize how wonderful God is to us.

> *Job 2:2-3, "And the Lord said to Satan, 'From where do you come?' So Satan answered the Lord and said, 'From going to and fro on the earth, and from walking back and forth on it.' Then the Lord said to Satan, 'Have you considered My servant Job, that there is none like him on the earth...?'"*

Do you really think God is going to be *incited* by the devil? Do you think God is going to let the devil intimidate Him and talk Him into doing something bad in your life just so He can prove how much faith you have in Him? No! That is not going to happen. Remember, God is a holy and just God. He is the Almighty, *not* satan. God is all powerful, satan is not. God does not care what satan says or thinks about anything.

> *Job 2:4-10,* "*So Satan answered the Lord and said, 'Skin for skin! Yes, all that a man has he will give for his life. But stretch out Your hand now, and touch his bone and his flesh, and he will surely curse You to Your face!' And the Lord said to Satan, 'Behold, he is in your hand, but spare his life.' So Satan went out from the presence of the Lord, and struck Job with painful boils from the sole of his foot to the crown of his head. And he took for himself a potsherd with which to scrape himself while he sat in the midst of the ashes. Then his wife said to him, 'Do you still hold fast to your integrity? Curse God and die!' But he said to her, 'You speak as one of the foolish women speaks. Shall we indeed accept good from God, and shall we not accept adversity?' In all this Job did not sin with his lips.*"

Here we see that Job had convinced himself that it was God who did both the good things in his life as well as the bad. If that were the kind of God we are serving, we would really be in a bad state of confusion.

CHAPTER TWELVE

The Fear of the Lord

There are a lot of hurting people out there, but there is good news. The Lord wants to help them! He has already paid the price for their pain, whether it is physical, emotional, or mental. All they have to do is believe it and receive it, and their lives will be transformed!

The more you are around people, the more you realize how many are hurting and searching for purpose in their lives—both rich and poor alike. The interesting thing is that both the rich and the poor are in the same boat if Jesus is not Lord of their lives—they are both going to hell when they die.

When you give your life to Jesus, make Him Lord and Master of your life, and get to know Him intimately, you have everything you need. You may think you need this and you may think you need that, but everything you need is found in Jesus Christ. When you know Him, you have no need for healing because He has already purchased your healing for you; you have no financial need because He has already called you blessed.

> *1 Corinthians 2:12, "Now we have received, not the spirit of the world, but the Spirit who is from God, that we might know the things that have been freely given to us by God."*

Do you know what has been freely given to you by God? God has given you eternal life, forgiveness of sins, healing, prosperity, and so much more. Your needs will be exceeded so you can be a blessing to the kingdom of God.

> *1 Corinthians 2:13-16,* *"These things we also speak, not in words which man's wisdom teaches but which the Holy Spirit teaches, comparing spiritual things with spiritual. But the natural man does not receive the things of the Spirit of God, for they are foolishness to him; nor can he know them, because they are spiritually discerned. But he who is spiritual judges all things, yet he himself is rightly judged by no one. For 'who has known the mind of the Lord that he may instruct Him?' But we have the mind of Christ."*

So He will instruct us, He will tell us what He desires, what He likes, what is wrong, what to do. He will share His revelation of things that we have no way of understanding or knowing, but we have to be in a place that we want to think like God and see things from His point of view.

We are expected to think like God, because as the Word says in Philippians 2:5, *"Let this mind be in you which was also in Christ Jesus."* When we read His Word, we need to agree with it. We may not understand it completely, but if our attitude about it is right and we have the desire to agree with His Word, then the understanding and revelation will come.

We are to see things from God's viewpoint. The natural man cannot do that, but the spiritual man can. God wants to reveal His secrets to us. When we get in agreement with His Word and desire to see things from His viewpoint, He will reveal His secrets to us. When we are in the Word and studying and fellowshipping with the Holy Spirit, He is going to reveal things to us in our prayer time; then when we attend church and hear the preacher say the same thing, we will be blessed and strengthened to know that the Lord had already told us the same thing. It will be a confirmation to us that we are in the right place and hearing from the Lord.

> *Ephesians 3:3-6 (Amp),* *"And that the mystery (secret) was made known to me and I was allowed to comprehend it by direct revelation, as I already briefly wrote you. When you read this you can understand my insight into the mystery of Christ. [This mystery] was never disclosed to human beings in past generations as it has now been revealed to His holy apostles [consecrated messengers] and prophets by the (Holy) Spirit. [It is this:] that the Gentiles are now to be fellow heirs [with the Jews], members of the same body and joint partakers (sharing) in the same*

divine promise in Christ through [their acceptance of] the glad tidings (the gospel)."

This is an example of revelation. When we spend time with God and seek Him, He reveals wonderful truths to us.

***Ephesians 3:12 (Amp)**, "In Whom, because of our faith in Him, we dare to have the boldness (courage and confidence) of free access—an unreserved approach to God with freedom and without fear."*

God wants us to come to Him and freely seek wisdom and understanding.

The Rich Man and Lazarus

In the following passage we see an account of two men who believed in God, but they had very different outcomes to their lives:

***Luke 16:19-31**, "There was a certain rich man who was clothed in purple and fine linen and fared sumptuously every day. But there was a certain beggar named Lazarus, full of sores, who was laid at his gate, desiring to be fed with the crumbs which fell from the rich man's table. Moreover the dogs came and licked his sores. So it was that the beggar died, and was carried by the angels to Abraham's bosom. The rich man also died and was buried. And being in torments in Hades, he lifted up his eyes and saw Abraham afar off, and Lazarus in his bosom. Then he cried and said, 'Father Abraham, have mercy on me, and send Lazarus that he may dip the tip of his finger in water and cool my tongue; for I am tormented in this flame.' But Abraham said, 'Son, remember that in your lifetime you received your good things, and likewise Lazarus evil things; but now he is comforted and you are tormented. and besides all this, between us and you there is a great gulf fixed, so that those who want to pass from here to you cannot, nor can those from there pass to us.' Then he said, 'I beg you therefore, father, that you would send him to my father's house, for I have five brothers, that he may testify to them, lest they also come to this place of torment.' Abraham said to him, 'They have Moses and the prophets; let them hear them.' And he said, 'No, father Abraham; but if one goes to them from the dead, they will repent.' But he said to him, 'If they do not hear Moses and the prophets, neither will they be persuaded though one rise from the dead.'"*

Abraham's bosom was a holding place for those who believed in God while they were on earth but had died before Jesus was crucified and resurrected from the dead. Hades was a holding place for those who died not believing in God. It was a place of torment, fire, and extreme unquenchable thirst, and never any relief. Plus there was a great impossible chasm fixed between the two holding places.

The reason Lazarus went to Abraham's bosom wasn't because he was sick but because he believed in God. Even though he was sickly and in poor condition he did not blame God; he believed in God and feared Him as well. We also see that the rich man died, but he went to Hades. Now a lot of people misconstrue that, saying, "See, having all that money caused this man to go to Hades." That is *not* what it is saying here! This man went to hell because he had no regard for the things of God.

This man who went to Hades called out to Father Abraham. This tells us that he was a Jew and knew who Abraham was. He was considered a believer in God by the standards at that time. Abraham knew this man because he called him "son." We have two things here that confirm that this man was a believer. Even though he was a believer in God, he did not do the things he was supposed to do. He was a man who had no regard for other people or the things of God. He even had five brothers like him; unmerciful, uncaring, unloving, they did not do what the Word of God said and were selfish.

There are a lot of people living today with that same disposition. Basically, they think that they are invincible and are not accountable to anyone for their actions. They cannot see beyond today. They think they are having fun and have no care about tomorrow or eternity.

Back in the time of this account of the rich man and Lazarus, the word of God was spoken by the prophets, so people knew it. Now, the rich man knew his brothers were just like him and needed to repent, but they would not do it unless there was some great, supernatural thing that happened in their lives. Abraham knew the heart of man, that even if someone would rise from the dead, they would not repent of their ways.

This is an awesome lesson for those of us who are still alive—we had better be paying attention and do what the Word of God is telling us to do.

Fear God.
The rich man's problem was not that he was so wealthy. I believe that his problem was that he did not fear God. He knew about God, but did not have a deep reverential awe for Him.

Had this rich man had the fear of God, he would have lived his life differently. When they brought Lazarus to his gate, he would have told one of his servants to make sure that he was given some food and to tend to the sores on his body. Who knows, maybe he would have even had Lazarus live in his house with him to make sure he was taken care of. That would be living your life with the fear of God, that deep reverential awe for God and His Word.

Everyone is going to give account to God for their life. It would have cost this rich man practically nothing to take care of Lazarus. The Word says that this rich man lived sumptuously, he had no lack. There was not anything that he wanted that he could not have.

I'm not talking about just doing good works, although that is something that we are supposed to do as Christians, but the important thing is that we fear God. If we fear God, we will view life from His point of view and consider, "What would God want me to do?" Well, He would certainly want us to do what Jesus did—heal the sick, cast out devils, feed the poor, help those people who are in need, and tell people about Him.

Here we see this rich man in never-ending torment for eternity! There is *not* any getting out of it. He ended up there simply because he had no fear of God.

What Is the Fear of God?

Defining the fear of God is much like trying to define the love of God; there are so many facets to it that it is difficult to sum it all up, but here are some ideas that may help:

1. It is having a deep reverential awe for God because of His sovereignty and love.

2. It is showing love for Him by shouting, singing, dancing, jumping—holding nothing back in expressing your deep love for Him.

3. It is having a selfless attitude about your life, knowing that your life belongs to Jesus, to love and serve Him with all your heart.

4. It is full acknowledgment that God is worthy of all praise, all worship, and any and all expression of love and adoration toward Him.

5. It is reverence, awe, and a total respect for God and His Word.

6. It is also the knowledge that God is a just God and *will* judge the living and the dead. He will judge us by how we lived our lives as Christians. He won't judge us for the nice things we did at the civic club or the flower show. Those are all admirable things to do, but God is going to judge us for how we lived before Him, how we viewed His Word, how we carried out His will for our lives, and how Christ-like we conducted ourselves.

Look at what the Word says in Malachi:

> *Malachi 3:14-18 (Amp), "You have said, It is useless to serve God, and what profit is it if we keep His ordinances and walk gloomily and as if in mourning apparel before the Lord of Hosts? And now we consider the proud and arrogant to be happy and favored; evildoers and exalted and prosper; yes, and when they test God, they escape [unpunished]. Then those who feared the Lord talked often one to another; and the Lord listened and heard it, and a book of remembrance was written before Him of those who reverenced and worshipfully feared the Lord and who thought on His name. And they shall be Mine, says the Lord of hosts, in that day when I publicly recognize and openly declare them to be my jewels–My special possession, My peculiar treasure. And I will spare them, as a man spares his own son who serves him. Then shall you return and discern between the righteous and the wicked, between him who serves God and him who does not serve Him."*

Some people have no understanding of God and no fear of Him either; they complain and accuse Him wrongly. In verse 16 we see what God says about those who fear Him. He has written a book of remembrance. The names of all the people who reverence Him, worship Him, fear Him, and think about Him are recorded in that book; they are the people God honors. In verse 17, we see that these same people will be publicly recognized and declared as God's jewels as well.

Totally saved

If you only had a casual conversion with the Lord, and you never were totally consumed with love for Jesus, you need to ask God to help you get to that point. You may need to go back to the Lord and tell Him that you missed something right from the beginning and that you want to renew your relationship with Him.

The longer you have been saved, the hotter you ought to be for Jesus. We are not to get saved and then just cool off. There is not a cool off period unless you allow it. It ought to always be a hot relationship. When you wake up in the morning, the Lord should be the very first thing on your mind.

What has been creeping into your heart and life that is causing you to lose the hot relationship you should have? Here is what the Lord said about having the fear of the Lord, it is the way to tell if you have the fear of God:

> **Deuteronomy 6:5,** *"You shall love the Lord your God with all your heart, with all your soul, and with all your strength."*

That is the fear of God; when you love Him with everything that identifies your whole being—your spirit, soul, and body—you love God with everything you are made up of. It is when you love God *all the time*, not just when things are going bad or you *really* want something from Him, and not just when things are going good. It is easy to love God when your bills are all paid. It's more of a challenge when they are not. You need to keep loving God and trusting Him, no matter what. When you are in that state, you are always burning hot in your relationship with God.

Be holy.
We are called to be a holy people. If you are indeed a Christian, a true believer, then you are expected by God, as well as other Christians, to live a holy and godly lifestyle—*all the time!*

> *1 Timothy 4:8*, *"For bodily exercise profits a little, but godliness is profitable for all things, having promise of the life that now is and of that which is to come."*

Godliness is being holy. Godliness is having the fear of God. Godliness is living like God and doing what His Word says.

Most people have a good revelation of the profitability of godliness, for when they die, they are escorted into heaven to spend all eternity there with Jesus. However, many do not realize that godliness, being holy, and having the fear of the Lord is also profitable for them right here and now. God says that being like Him, being in agreement with Him, thinking like Him, loving His Word, speaking His Word, being like Jesus (which *is* possible), is going to profit you right now.

The word "life" in the Greek is *zoë* and it speaks of quality of life and abundance. So the Word says that godliness is profitable for a quality of abundant life now, that you will have the favor of God on you. Yes, we are saved by grace, not by our own works. But as we maintain and continue to live in godliness, there is a reward. There is profitability.

Nobody becomes saved because they think they are going to be rich and successful. You were saved because you were miserable, hurting, and you realized you were damned to eternal death in hell. You knew that you had no hope and that you needed Jesus Christ. Then after you were saved and knew that your sins were forgiven, you started to read the Word. That is when you realized that there is a lot more to being saved than going to heaven when you die, and you wanted to find out everything the Word has to say about your life on earth as well as your eternal life. So the quest began to know God more intimately. However, if you ever lose that love for God and the fear of God, and start treating Him casually, you will slowly lose all that God has promised you in His Word.

What has happened in a lot of denominational churches is that the Holy Spirit is simply not there anymore. The people are just going through the motions of being a Christian, just trying to do something to make it look good. What they really need is a relationship with God and to develop the fear of the Lord in their life again. They need to fall in love with Him again and live a godly lifestyle, and then their lives will change for the better.

When I became saved, I automatically had the fear of God. I knew where I was, what I was about, where I was going, and all of a sudden I realized I was not going to hell anymore! God saved me! That was such a great revelation. I had so much joy and peace. I thank God every day for saving me. I have this fear, this reverential awe of God's sovereignty, and the fear of doing wrong against Him, of saying the wrong thing, and of sinning. I do not want to be judged for knowingly doing wrong.

Those who give their lives to Jesus but continue to willfully sin, thinking that it is okay because they can just go back and ask Jesus to forgive them, are in a bad place. I am not saying that God will not forgive them, but they are putting God to a foolish test. There is no fear of God in them if they think they can keep living like that.

It is sad to know that so many pastors are preaching that God is just this big sugar daddy who does not really care what you do, and that He understands why you live like the ungodly and will love you anyway.

You are in God's family.
Being a child of God is like being a child in any family. There are consequences when a child goes against his parents' will. It is the same in God's family; there are consequences when you disobey God and His Word. If you fear God *and* fear those consequences, you are going to do all you can to live right before Him and not go off and do your own thing. You should not have the spirit of the world still residing in you. If you do, you need to get rid of it! If you have something in your life, your desires, or your actions that has a hold on you that is not holy, and you still want to dabble in it, you do not have the fear of God. You *need* to come to the place where you fear God—you fear the just and righteous Judge.

Matthew 10:27-28, "Whatever I tell you in the dark, speak in the light; and what you hear in the ear, preach on the housetops. And do not fear those who kill the body but cannot kill the soul. But rather fear Him who is able to destroy both soul and body in hell."

You are not to fear man, you are to fear God! Man may be able to kill you, but they cannot keep your soul out of heaven. You have to determine in your own heart if you are going to serve the world, serve man, serve your own fleshly desires, or if you are going to serve God. The choice is yours, only you can make it.

God knows if you are just giving Him lip service or if you are giving Him true heart service. If you are surrendered and submitted to Him, He knows that. He also knows if you are struggling with something, and He is always there to help you. He doesn't laugh at you, ignore you, or abandon you. He wants to help you to live right.

You will be tempted.
Rest assured that even if you are a Christian who fears God wholeheartedly, you will have all kinds of temptations come your way. The devil will work overtime to try to get you to stumble and turn your back on God. He may not be able to keep you out of heaven, but he sure can hinder you from having a close, intimate relationship with God and doing mighty exploits for His kingdom. God has made a way of escape:

1 Corinthians 10:13, "No temptation has overtaken you except such as is common to man; but God is faithful, who will not allow you to be tempted beyond what you are able, but with the temptation will also make the way of escape, that you may be able to bear it."

When you call upon His name, He will be there to deliver you and help you:

Psalm 91:14-16, "Because he has set his love upon Me, therefore I will deliver him; I will set him on high, because he has known My name. He shall call upon Me, and I will answer him; I will be with him in trouble; I will deliver him and honor him; with long life I will satisfy him, and show him My salvation."

The devil will relentlessly bombard us with lies about who we are and who we are not. However, God has given us weapons to fight those attacks. He has given us His Word and His authority over the devil in Jesus' name. We need to *use* them!

The Fear of the Lord Is a Catalyst for Your Faith

God has already done the most costly thing for you by giving His only begotten Son to die for your sins so that you do not have to pay the penalty for them. Don't you think He will help you in everything else then? But you need to have the fear of God in order for your faith to operate properly.

> *Luke 23:39-43, "Then one of the criminals who were hanged blasphemed Him, saying, 'If You are the Christ, save Yourself and us.' But the other, answering, rebuked him, saying, 'Do you not even fear God, seeing you are under the same condemnation? And we indeed justly, for we receive the due reward of our deeds; but this Man has done nothing wrong.' Then he said to Jesus, 'Lord, remember me when You come into Your kingdom.' And Jesus said to him, 'Assuredly, I say to you, today you will be with Me in Paradise.'"*

Here we see Jesus hanging on a cross between two sinners. It was a gross, horrible, horrendous, shameful, painful, embarrassing, and humiliating crucifixion of the Son of God. Anybody that would do that for you, you had better listen to, respect, and be in awe of!

One of the thieves had absolutely no fear of God. He knew who Jesus was, but even in his last dying moments he still had no respect for God. However, the other criminal *did* have the fear of God. This man did not say a formal sinner's prayer, but what came out of his heart was all that was needed because he truly feared God.

> *Acts 9:28-31, "So he was with them at Jerusalem, coming in and going out. And he spoke boldly in the name of the Lord Jesus and disputed against the Hellenists, but they attempted to kill him. When the brethren found out, they brought him down to Caesarea and sent him out to Tarsus. Then the churches throughout all Judea, Galilee, and Samaria had peace and were edified. And walking in the fear of the Lord and in the comfort of the Holy Spirit, they were multiplied."*

When they were walking in the fear of the Lord, they were multiplied! Paul preached Christ *boldly!* He preached the same message that the apostles preached because he had been caught up into the heavenlies and he had been instructed by Jesus Himself. He proclaimed the same things as the apostles who actually walked with Jesus for three years! Paul knew everything that the apostles knew and he was preaching it with great boldness.

Here's the key: Speak boldly in the name of the Lord Jesus Christ, walk in the fear of the Lord, and then the comfort of the Holy Spirit will be upon you. You have to be bold in your faith. If you are being tempted, becoming weak, and having trouble, then you need to step up and start to preach. Start preaching Christ and what He did for you. God will then do a work in you. That boldness is like a defense against the enemy. When he hears what you are preaching and testifying to, he cannot get near you. But if you are weak, cowardly, and ashamed to say that you are a Christian then the devil has access to you. Be bold!

Get wisdom because you do have the mind of Christ.

Psalm 111:10a, "*The fear of the Lord is the beginning of wisdom.*"

1 Corinthians 2:16, "*For 'who has known the mind of the Lord that he may instruct Him?' But we have the mind of Christ.*"

Philippians 2:15, "*Let this mind be in you which was also in Christ Jesus.*"

When you get the wisdom of God, then everything else will come to you. You start to fear the Lord, respect Him, and see Him as the source of all good things, then He will give you wisdom to accomplish things for His kingdom and you will have peace and joy in your life. God is all about you having peace, comfort, joy, and all your needs met and exceeded. He is not about you suffering, because He has already done all the suffering for you!

If you have the mind of Christ, then you are going to have the fear of God and see things from His point of view. Again, there are many Christians who say they love the Lord, but they really do not have the "fear of God" and they are living as such.

If that rich man in Luke 16 would have asked what God would have him do, I believe things would have turned out differently for him. He believed in God, but did not have the fear of God. What a price to pay—eternity in hell for refusing to obey the Lord and fear God!

The fear of God is a 24/7 state of being. The fear of God originates from your spirit man because that is where the Holy Spirit speaks to you from. When you have the fear of the Lord, He is always foremost in your mind. In order to accomplish that, you have to make a conscious effort to keep your spirit man in charge and your soul and flesh subject to your spirit man. Then you will be walking in the fear of God day-in and day-out.

Never Flirt With Sin

Some so-called Christians are trying to live as close to sin as they can without getting burned. They are flirting with sin, trying to get as close as possible to sin and still be saved. They go right to the edge and dabble just a little bit, then go back to what is right. Then a little while later they go to the edge again and dabble a little more, and then go back. They keep doing that until one day they dabble too much and fall off that edge and right into full-blown sin.

You cannot be living on the edge of your salvation all the time. When you continually live on the edge of your salvation, by dabbling in your sinful desires and not having the fear of the Lord, do not be surprised if your life becomes a mess and you do not have the favor of God flowing in it anymore. If you are comfortable with living on the edge of your salvation and you are not feeling guilty and ashamed, if you can actually enjoy yourself while you are in the middle of sinning, I really wonder if you are actually saved.

I have gone into bars and cast out devils and preached the gospel. I was uncomfortable, but I had boldness to preach. I'll do it again as the Lord leads, but to just go to a bar and sit there drinking a cola and hanging out is not a godly virtue. If you go to the bar, you'd better be there to tell them about Jesus. The Spirit of God is not comfortable in places of sin unless He has sent you there on assignment.

If you are comfortable in the sin you are actively involved in, either you are not really saved, or your conscience has been seared, meaning that your conscience cannot convict you anymore because it has become so deadened.

I see so many people in the body of Christ who are always getting into trouble. They are always backpedaling, backsliding, dabbling with a little bit of sin, and then getting right again. That is not the way the Christian life is supposed to be lived. That is a pretty low way of living.

One day I asked the Lord why it is that some people are born again, live straight as an arrow, and keep going on steadily for God even in the midst of problems and temptations; at the same time there are others who claim they are Christians and are falling off the wagon, tumbling into ditches, tripping over every little pothole that comes their way in life, and succumbing to every little temptation that presents itself? Why is it that there seems to be these two kinds of people: those who claim to be Christians and are living Christ-like and holy, and those who claim to be Christians, but are living unholy like the rest of the world? It cannot be both ways!

The Holy Spirit answered my question when He said, "Those who live victorious, holy lives have a reverence of me. Those who like to flirt with sin and live dirty lack a fear and reverence of Me."

Either you are saved, living like Christ, thinking like Him, agreeing with Him, and seeing life from His point of view, or you are way out in left field, saying you are a Christian but doing everything else *but* living like Christ. You are into unholy relationships, fornication, drinking, drugs, pornography, lying, cheating, gossiping, and then you go to the house of God on Sunday and act all holy. Do you think you are fooling God? You might be fooling the people around you for awhile, but not God!

I used to be a Christian.
Here is an example of what I am talking about. I was praying as I was coming home from church one Wednesday night, and the Lord showed me a certain intersection in downtown Oshkosh, Wisconsin. At the time I lived about 20 miles from there.

The Lord said, "I want you to go there in the morning and I will tell what to do when you get there." I woke up in the morning thinking, *Man, I've got an assignment from God.* I just love having an assignment from God because you never know what is going to happen.

I drove down there and parked my car at the intersection I saw in the vision, but I was not exactly sure yet what I was supposed to do. It was a cold, blustery March morning with not many people out. I decided to find somebody and give them a tract. I went into the stores and handed out tracts and talked to people. I knew God had something more for me to do, but I just was not hearing Him.

So, I went to the vantage point that I saw of the intersection in the vision to see if I could see what God was trying to show me. I went across the street to a little park bench and sat there. I looked across the street and there it was—some kind of an adult bookstore right downtown! It was like a plague in that whole area.

I saw that and I said, "Oh no, Lord, You don't want me going in there, that isn't good! What if somebody *sees* me?" Well, I did not go marching right over there…no, I went marching the other way, pleading with the Lord not to make me go in!

Finally I yielded. I asked the Lord to help me and to show me exactly what to do. I walked over and as I put my hand on the door, the Lord spoke to me and said, "Ask for the manager and tell them I love them." I pictured some big burly motorcycle guy with chains, tattoos, and a Mohawk haircut picking me up and throwing me out, but I knew God was with me. I walked in and it was like blinders came along side my eyes, and I had tunnel vision. I only saw what I needed to see. But wouldn't you know it? The desk was way at the back of the store, so I had to walk all the way through the store to get to it.

If you want to get a rush, if you want to get a Holy Ghost fire burning in you, go out on an assignment. I will never forget it. I was on fire! The glory of God was on me and I was just burning up. I felt like, *Let me at the devil. I am here. I am ready. I have no fear. I am not tempted by anything.*

I walked back to that counter and asked for the manager. This young 20 year old girl said, "Yeah, I'm the manager." I thought, *Praise God! I'm going to live and not die today!*

The Lord had showed me a couple of Scriptures to share and so I said, "You don't know me, but last night as I was praying God spoke to me and told me to come here and to tell you that He loves you and He wants me to share His Word with you."

I stood there in this pornographic book store and read the Word of God to her. People were going back and forth to the peep shows, and some were being waited on at the counter by other clerks. I just stood there and read out of the gospel of John.

She put her cigarette down and froze right there. She could not move. She was arrested by the Holy Ghost. When I was all done, she said, "Sir, I used to be a Christian." (Those are the saddest words that one can hear—I used to be a Christian; I used to go to Sunday school and Youth Group; I used to love the Lord; I was born again, and then I started to do some things with my friends…) "But last night," she continued, "as I was lying on my bed, I cried to God and prayed, 'Lord, if You can forgive me and You still love me, send someone to tell me.'"

I will never forget those words. I felt very humbled that God had sent me out of the thousands of Christians who lived in that area. I encourage each of you to stay close to God, fear Him, and always make yourself available for God's will to be done through you because you will miss out on some very exciting times if you don't.

The Lord had given me a word of knowledge, and I told her that the Lord knew all the men that she had slept with and that He forgave her, but that she needed to surrender her life to Him. So, she knew that I knew things about her.

She said that little by little she had just drifted away from God. The little temptations came in over a period of time and she drifted off. She ended up being like a ship without a rudder in the middle of the ocean. We shared back and forth with each other, I prayed for her, and she came back to the Lord.

This woman's love for God had drifted away. She went from being a born again teenager who loved God to becoming the manager of a pornographic book store. The fear of God was no longer in her life. Backsliding like that is a horrible thing and it goes on all the time… "I used to be a Christian, but little by little I started doing things and drifting away from God…"

Those who dabble in sin and think they are still okay are being greatly deceived! They are being fools! Do not accept what your Christian peers are doing if it is ungodly. Tell them that they need to get right with Jesus again. Living like the world is not the way God has called us to live. It is not acceptable to the Lord. I do not care what modern theology is telling you or what some churches are preaching. God does *not* condone sin no matter why you keep doing it. He has already done everything He could to keep you out of it, but you choose to go back into it.

There are so many lost and hurting people out there who would believe in Jesus if someone who knew Him would just take the time to share about Him. Be willing and obedient to tell others of Jesus. That is God's number one thing for us to do.

The before and after difference
Before you were born again, sinning was hard on your body and your life. It messed up your mind, it messed up relationships, it messed up your body, and it stole your money—it was hard. You had no joy, no peace, and you had to keep taking drugs and/or alcohol to try to get happy, but that wears off and leaves you broke, with a headache, and sick. You used to puke like a dog, thinking you were having fun. You would smoke dope until your eyeballs rolled back in your head, and you could hardly breathe, but *man* that was fun! Oh, really?

> ***1 Peter 1:13,*** *"Therefore gird up the loins of your mind, be sober, and rest your hope fully upon the grace that is to be brought to you at the revelation of Jesus Christ."*

So when you were born again and received Christ as your Lord and Savior, the grace of God was given to you. But we need to be sober and serious about the things of God; we are not to be loose and liberal, thinking you can do whatever pleases *you*. God is a holy God and a revelation that you need to have is that Jesus Christ is holy, perfect, and pure. You need to watch what comes out of your mouth and be careful about what you are thinking.

> *1 Peter 1:14-16, "As obedient children, not conforming yourselves to the former lusts, as in your ignorance; but as He who called you is holy, you also be holy in all your conduct, because it is written, 'Be holy, for I am holy.'"*

I like that word "all," it actually does mean *all!* We are to be holy in *all* our conduct; it does not say in most of it. Everything you do ought to be holy! Everything you do ought to be set apart unto God. To be holy means to be in total agreement with God and His ways, and to *do* what His Word says. It is not legalism; it is not about how you wear your hair or what clothes you wear. To be holy means to be like God; it means to have the mind of God, to think like Him, and not argue with His Word.

> *1 Peter 1:17, "And if you call on the Father, who without partiality judges according to each one's work, conduct yourselves throughout the time of your stay here in fear."*

That is reverential awe. As you recall, in Matthew 10:28, Jesus said that we are not to fear what can kill the body, but we are to fear Him who can cast our soul into hell. God is the ultimate, righteous judge.

> *1 Peter 1:18, "Knowing that you were not redeemed with corruptible things, like silver or gold, from your aimless conduct received by tradition from your fathers, but with the precious blood of Christ, as of a lamb without blemish and without spot."*

Peter is talking about the Jewish religion and man's rules and laws. We were redeemed by a Holy God.

Jesus Christ was holy and blameless. Isn't that amazing? He lived thirty-three years on the earth and never sinned, yet He was found to be a man in every way. He had to be sinless, blameless, and holy in order to be the Perfect Sacrifice for us.

Having No Fear of God Is Detrimental to Your Life

In Numbers 16 we find the account of Korah. He and a couple of partners decided one day that Moses was too powerful, had too much authority, and that they were going to take Moses down a notch or two. So they gathered about 250 men together and came to Moses and Aaron and challenged them. They must have forgotten that God had called Moses and Aaron to lead them out of Egypt. God had also called these other men to help Moses and Aaron, but He had not given them the same position and level of authority as He had given Moses and Aaron. Moses was the leader, the man in charge. Aaron was the chief priest. When you read that account you can see that they did not have the fear of God. They had religious ideas and mind-sets, but not the fear of God.

The spirit of religion can come on you quickly. When you get away from Jesus, you get all kinds of religion. When the Holy Spirit departs, man will fill up the church services with religion. They are trying to "look" godly as though they are serving God in all their rituals, but they are only serving themselves because the Holy Spirit has departed from their midst.

You do not ever want to be separated from the Holy Spirit. I meet Christians who talk religious, they sound like they are born again, but they are falling short of the mark because they are only "trying" to look godly. We need to be discerning about this. We should look past what people are saying and doing, and see them how the Holy Spirit sees them so that we will not be fooled by them.

Korah and his men came to Moses telling him that they wanted him to step down so that they could step up. Here are some of the things that Korah was mad about: (1) He thought he should be the chief priest rather than Aaron. (2) He thought that Moses had too much authority and that some of that authority should be spread out among his friends. They wanted to give the orders, to be in charge. (3) He was angry because he was not going to go into the Promised Land—but that was because of the sin of the people; ten of them came back with an evil report because *they* did not fear God, and the people believed them instead of the two who *did* fear God and had *His* report. These ten had no fear of God's word and were going against what God had said.

If you do not believe what God's Word says, then you do not have the fear of God. If you fear God, you are going to believe His Word.

Here we have this rebellion by Korah and his men, and Moses goes before the Lord. He said that the next day He was going to decide between them. The next day Moses and everybody were out by their tents, and God said for everybody not in agreement with Korah and his men to get away from their tents. They were not to associate with them.

> *Numbers 16:31-38, "Now it came to pass, as he finished speaking all these words, that the ground split apart under them, and the earth opened its mouth and swallowed them up, with their households and all the men with Korah, with all their goods. So they and all those with them went down alive into the pit; the earth closed over them, and they perished from among the assembly. Then all Israel who were around them fled at their cry, for they said, 'Lest the earth swallow us up also!' And a fire came out from the Lord and consumed the two hundred and fifty men who were offering incense. Then the Lord spoke to Moses, saying: 'Tell Eleazar, the son of Aaron the priest, to pick up the censers out of the blaze, for they are holy, and scatter the fire some distance away. The censers of these men who sinned against their own souls, let them be made into hammered plates as a covering for the altar. Because they presented them before the Lord, therefore they are holy; and they shall be a sign to the children of Israel.'"*

Korah was a covenant breaker with a spirit of divorce. Divorce is not only about marriages breaking up; divorce is about the breaking of covenant. That is why Jesus said He hates divorce; He knew it was a spirit that broke covenant as well as relationships.

Anyone who ends up in hell will see Korah and those 250 men down there. They will be there because they chose not to have the fear of God. We need to *always* be in the place where we are in total awe of God and love the Lord. Wherever there is a lack of fear of God, sin creeps in; it slowly slithers right into our lives.

Familiarity can lead to not fearing God.
While in the garden of Eden, Eve had to have let her guard down. Adam

and Eve had such an awesome position and relationship with God. They actually walked with God in the cool of the day! Man has been trying to do that ever since. As born again Christians, we have that relationship in the spirit realm, but with them it was in the natural realm too!

Adam and Eve essentially divorced themselves from God and joined themselves to satan. Those who do not maintain a healthy fear of God will open the door for that very thing to happen to them. "Familiarity breeds contempt." When you get to know somebody too well you get too casual with them. I believe both Adam and Eve became too casual with God—they lost that fear of Him.

When satan came to Eve, he had another message. Eve knew what God had done and what He had said, but she had lost that fear so she believed what the devil said; she believed another message.

Because of their disobedience and lack of the fear of God, mankind has been damned ever since. They lost that love, respect, and reverential awe for God and started to take Him too casually. It happens to many Christians today. They start thinking of Him as their buddy, their chum. Yes, we are to have a close intimate relationship with our heavenly Father, but at the same time we need to hold Him in total and complete reverential awe.

Those who stop having the fear of God will stop living holy lives and will start living carnal lives with a little religion added in. God's presence stops going with you when you stop fearing Him.

Moses had a fear of God and so God's presence remained with him. Abraham had a fear of God; he messed up along the way, but got right with Him again and God went with him.

King Saul started out fearing God, but as he lost that fear, he began to fear man and started to sin and give his own sacrifices. If you fear man more than you fear God, you are going to lose your relationship with God. You *have* to fear God and be deeply and completely in love with Him.

The Fear of the Lord

Live right, live holy, live godly; it is profitable!
This message is what every Christian and non-Christian needs to hear. You need to have the fear of God, you need to determine to love God with all that is in you and not let the lies of the devil creep in and deceive you into losing your intimate relationship with God! Do not drift away. Stop trying to live at the very edge of your salvation.

> ***Psalm 34:7,*** *"The angel of the Lord encamps all around those who fear Him, and delivers them."*

If you need to be delivered from something, you had better get back to fearing God! You had better fall in love with God all over again. If you have *any* kind of problem in your life—*fear God!*

> ***Psalm 34:8,*** *"Oh, taste and see that the Lord is good; blessed is the man who trusts in Him!"*

That means happy and prosperous. It is profitable to fear God.

> ***Psalm 34:9-15,*** *"Oh, fear the Lord, you His saints! There is no want to those who fear Him. The young lions lack and suffer hunger; but those who seek the Lord shall not lack any good thing. Come, you children, listen to me; I will teach you the fear of the Lord. Who is the man who desires life, and loves many days, that he may see good? Keep your tongue from evil, and your lips from speaking deceit. Depart from evil and do good; seek peace and pursue it. The eyes of the Lord are on the righteous, and His ears are open to their cry."*

This is not a condemning message for anyone; the only thing that will ever condemn someone is sin and wrong living. This message should lift us up and point us in the right direction. It will remind us that we can all live at the level God has called us to live. We can live like the redeemed of the Lord. We can live like a new creation in Jesus. We can live like we are the righteousness of God in Christ Jesus. We are a chosen generation, a royal priesthood—but we *must* have the fear of the Lord operating in our lives at all times.

CHAPTER THIRTEEN

What To Do When Trouble Comes

Trials and Tribulations

In the books of James and 1 Peter, it says that we won't be tested beyond what we can handle. That does *not* mean that God sends tests and trials to us. Yes, tests and trials come because we live in this world. We realize our need for God and how we need to get our faith strong in Him. When handled properly, tests and trials can bring us to the place of strength in our relationship with God where we do not cave in when trials and tribulations come.

Our U. S. Marines are the best trained soldiers in the world, but until they face the real enemy, they do not know how well their training has prepared them. Tests, trials, and battles are what help develop our faith and trust in God's Word. When a trial comes our way, we should not cry and run from it. We should shout the Word of God and run *at* it!

God knows that we are going to have tests and trials. Jesus said in the Word that we will have tribulations, but we are not to fear because He has overcome the world. He did not say that He sent those trials to us. God is not sitting around planning what trials and troubles He wants to send into our lives.

The devil has a plan to destroy your life, and all kinds of tests and trials are going to come. This is what brings confusion into the body of Christ.

What To Do When Trouble Comes

When a bad situation arises or sickness comes, right away people think, "Oh, is God testing me? If so, what am I supposed to do about this? Am I supposed to pray and ask for this to go away?" He would be a very sick god if He put something bad on you and then told you to pray about it to see if you have a good enough prayer and enough faith to get that sickness or situation off you.

Our God does not work like that, but He knows that the devil wants to do things to us. He also knows that He has paid the price for our deliverance and has given us authority in the name of Jesus. He has also given us the blood of Jesus and the power of prayer so we can bind up the devil and keep him under our feet. At the same time, we can receive the love and mercy of God along with the wonderful things God has in store for us. So many people in the body of Christ have not figured this out yet. They are still struggling with it. It is time to get it established.

Pray the Word

When faced with difficult trials, many Christians do not know what to pray. They have the mind-set that if it is God's will, you should not pray about it. If God sent you sickness to test your faith then you should take that sickness, live with it, and die with it because if God sent you something and you are praying to get rid of it, then you are in rebellion to God. As I have said before, that is *not* how God works.

When sickness, trouble, or whatever begins coming into your life, the Holy Spirit is right there encouraging you to take authority over it, build your faith, press in to the presence of God, and become more mature because of it. The Holy Ghost will begin to bring to your remembrance Scriptures pertaining to the situation. Use them continually. Speak them out until you see your answer in the natural realm. But before He can bring to our remembrance the Word of God, we have to have it in our spirit and in our understanding as well. That is why it is so important to read His Word, pray, praise, and spend quality time with the Holy Spirit on a consistent, daily basis.

> *Matthew 16:19, "And I will give you the keys of the kingdom of heaven, and whatever you bind on earth will be bound in heaven, and whatever you loose on earth will be loosed in heaven."*

If Jesus told us that we have authority over satan, that things we bind on earth are bound in heaven, that what we forbid in the earth is backed up by God Himself, then we had better believe it and use it! If God is allowing things to come on us, then why did Jesus tell us to bind those things up and rebuke the devil? If that were the case, this would be a house divided against itself, which would not stand.

We are the ones who allow those things to come into our lives because we either do not know the Word, or we get lazy and stop praying fervently as we should. When something comes, sometimes it is just easier to receive it than it is to fight against it. God wants us to exercise our faith by fighting against it in the spirit realm and with His Word. Jesus already paid the price on the cross. He has already given us all the power and authority that comes with His name to keep satan under our feet and inactive active in our lives. We need to operate in that so it becomes our lifestyle.

Do you realize that God sees what is coming and tries to get us to pray against it even before it arrives? But He cannot do anything in the spirit realm unless we do our part. It is up to us to ward off the devil's attacks. And once we have been attacked, we have to do our part to get rid of it.

The mind-set that "God giveth and God taketh away" is not true. God gave to Job in the beginning of the book, and He gave him a double portion at the end!

When someone believes the doctrine that God sends us evil to teach us things—pray for that individual! We do not go around afflicting our own children just to see how they will handle it; why would God do that to us? Our children oftentimes bring on their troubles because of their own actions, but we never inflict sickness and trials on them to teach them something!

Yes, Jesus said that tests and trials will come our way, not because He sent them, but because we open a door somewhere in our lives for the devil to get in. But what did Jesus say *about* those tests and trials? He said that He has made a way of escape, and He has given us everything we need to keep satan under our feet and live a victorious life. He gave us all these things for us to exercise them in our lives and operate in them. When we do so, we bring glory to the heavenly Father!

When we pray the Word of God over situations in our lives and take authority over the devil, we build our faith in God; we live a life that brings glory to Him. How can anyone think that living a beat-down, poverty-stricken, grovel-in-the-dirt type lifestyle could ever bring glory to God?

CHAPTER FOURTEEN

Summary

I have told you the truth in this book. God spoke to me for ten days about the book of Job. He woke me in the middle of the night and talked to me. He said, "For all these years people have had this all twisted around. They thought Job was some saint, some wonderful person."

People have said, "Oh, if we could just be like Job. If we could just have some destruction come in our life, we could be like him." Quite a warped sense of God from my point of view!

> *James 5:11, "Indeed we count them blessed who endure. You have heard of the perseverance of Job and seen the end intended by the Lord—that the Lord is very compassionate and merciful."*

James said Job persevered, and the *end* intended by the Lord was God's desire for Job to know Him personally and to know that God did not give satan permission to do all those wicked things to him. The Lord also restored everything, and even doubled it when Job repented for his false ideas of God.

> *Job 42:5-6, "I have heard of You by the hearing of the ear, but now my eye sees You. Therefore I abhor myself, and repent in dust and ashes."*

Our ministry is to set the captives of satan free; we are to bring them from darkness into light.

Here is a summary of the mistakes Job made:

Summary

1. He claimed to be a righteous man.

2. He claimed he was a pure man.

3. He claimed he had not sinned.

4. He did not know of anything that he had done wrong.

5. He said that God had done all this to him and he did not understand why.

This is the essence of the first part of the book of Job. So, when did Job say what was right about God? The first and only time we see that Job spoke correctly about God was in Job 42:4-6. He did not speak the truth about God for 41 chapters before that.

> *Job 42:8, "Now therefore, take for yourselves seven bulls and seven rams, go to My servant Job, and offer up for yourselves a burnt offering; and My servant Job shall pray for you. For I will accept him, lest I deal with you according to your folly; because you have not spoken of Me what is right, as My servant Job has."*

Why did God accept Job? Because he repented. Job became saved. He got rid of religion and became a believer. God was saying that Job and his three friends were all in the same boat, but Job repented. Now it was these three guys' turn to do the same.

> *Job 42:10-13, "And the Lord restored Job's losses when he prayed for his friends. Indeed the Lord gave Job twice as much as he had before. Then all his brothers, all his sisters, and all those who had been his acquaintances before, came to him and ate food with him in his house; and they consoled him and comforted him for all the adversity that the Lord had brought upon him. Each one gave him a piece of silver and each a ring of gold. Now the Lord blessed the latter days of Job more than his beginning; for he had fourteen thousand sheep, six thousand camels, one thousand yoke of oxen, and one thousand female donkeys. He also had seven sons and three daughters."*

Wow! Look what repentance can do. The book of Job is actually a very awesome book when read and understood *God's* way. When this book is viewed from God's perspective, and not from man's perspective or from a religious perspective, it has an entirely new meaning. The Word of God has proven that Job was not all that he thought he was at the beginning of the book of Job. It has also proven what happens when someone encounters God and truly repents of his errors.

So, now you know how to answer people when they try to convince you of their doctrine that God sends adversity our way to teach or test us based on what it says in the book of Job. Job was wrong! He made a *big* mistake about God's nature and His ways. The only difference between Job and a lot of Christians these days is that *Job repented for not knowing what he was talking about!* Oh, that all Christians would do the same today.

God allowed the Book of Job to be written from Job's wrong perspective so those who read it would see Job's mistake and not make the same mistake of blaming God for their troubles.

About the Author

Billy Ferg is a pastor, apostle, and author who has written several other successful books. His desire as a Christian leader is to help the Body of Christ have victory in their lives, understand who they are in Christ, and find their place in God's plan. Billy has traveled to thirty countries where he has held large crusades bringing messages of hope, healing, and deliverance to the masses. He has a heart for God's people, the local church, and pastors, which are the backbone of strong nations. Where the light of God's Word shines, the righteous are in charge.

To contact the author, please write:
Living Faith Ministries
P.O. Box 16226
Duluth MN 55816